I0062524

DECODING

BODY

LANGUAGE

SECRETS

MASTER NONVERBAL CUES, ENHANCE
COMMUNICATION SKILLS, AND THRIVE
IN PERSONAL AND PROFESSIONAL
RELATIONSHIPS

SkillSet Mastery Publications

TABLE OF CONTENTS

INTRODUCTION

THERE IS A GROWING NEED TO UNDERSTAND THE PEOPLE WE INTERACT with daily. From business associates to employees, colleagues, clients, and prospects – these people virtually form our professional world. Studies have shown that the average person spends over 90,000 hours of their lifetime at work, emphasizing the profound impact of these interactions on our lives. We must actively seek to improve our relationships with them to boost our businesses or careers and enhance our overall well-being and satisfaction.

However, with the many complexities associated with human behavior, understanding the many different individuals in our professional lives is a very daunting task for many people. And as if that is not difficult enough, the pace at which technology affects human interaction makes our people-reading skills less sharp. Technology has produced a lot of online communication "experts" who cannot even maintain eye contact with a stranger in real life, let alone observe them long enough to read their body language accurately.

Some individuals have long desired to acquire the fundamental knowledge necessary for enhancing their communication skills, allowing them to excel in their personal relationships and career interactions with clients and prospects. Even with this, they may prefer to avoid the challenge of undertaking the required to understand human psychology, citing various reasons for their hesitation.

Many, too, have found that they must deal with difficult people in the workplace, which can be very challenging and draining. It is like sucking the life out of them each time they must contact such difficult people.

In this book, we have taken the time to outline, in simple terms, the skills, steps, and tips that will help you improve your ability to understand people and effectively interact with them. What you need to know about body language, human psychology, and how personality affects business are all explained here. If you have difficulty understanding how to match people's words with their body language, this book will expose you to that information. You will also learn to show others that you see things from their unique point of view.

Building strong connections and fostering genuine relationships is essential for your career and personal life. When you cultivate strong relationships with clients, employees, and employers, the positive outcomes transcend your career and personal life, impacting every facet of your existence. Whether in professional or personal settings, these steps are crucial for establishing lasting connections with the individuals who hold significance in your life.

Often, our failure to comprehend the intricacies of human psychology and interpret evident nonverbal cues can result in misdirected efforts toward individuals with little interest in us or what we offer.

Within the pages of this book, you will uncover valuable insights on deciphering signs of both interest and disinterest when engaging in conversations. Additionally, you will acquire helpful techniques for skillfully addressing objections and leveraging them to your advantage.

Moreover, this book delves into the fundamental principles of presenting your best self in any encounter, including initial meetings, ensuring a solid foundation for successful interactions.

WHO WE ARE

SkillSet Mastery Publications is your gateway to unlocking the secrets of mastering the art of reading body language. Our sole purpose is to equip individuals with the knowledge and skills necessary to excel in personal relationships, business endeavors, career advancements, and profound connections with others.

Recognizing the immense significance of non-verbal communication in every interaction, SkillSet Mastery Publications, our goal is to offer you practical and insightful resources that help you uncover the hidden messages conveyed through body language. We dedicate ourselves to equipping you with the tools and knowledge to understand non-verbal communication better.

Whether you aspire to ace job interviews, enhance your sales prowess, or delve into the captivating world of non-verbal cues, our publications cater to various interests.

We firmly believe in fostering positive learning experiences. Our book emphasizes constructive techniques and strategies that empower you to effectively interpret and leverage body language. Through our materials, you will learn to discern subtle gestures, decode facial expressions, and decipher postures, enabling you to navigate social dynamics with unwavering confidence and precision.

Join SkillSet Mastery Publications on a transformative journey, where you will unlock the profound potential nestled within the realm of body language.

WHO IS THIS BOOK FOR

This book targets individuals interested in improving their communication skills, understanding human behavior, and building successful relationships, particularly in professional settings. The book covers topics such as analyzing people, handling objections and resistance, reading non-verbal cues, understanding different personality types, advanced human psychology, reading basic body language, the power of the handshake, using eye signals, building rapport, and advanced forms of body language reading.

The chapters provide practical advice, techniques, and insights for individuals who want to enhance their ability to communicate effectively, navigate social interactions, and understand the underlying motivations and intentions of others. The target audience may include professionals in sales, business, leadership, or any field where interpersonal skills and understanding human behavior are crucial. Individuals interested in psychology, self-improvement, and personal development may also find value in the book.

So, prepare to embark on a transformative journey into decoding the "Silent Language," a language often expressed but seldom truly heard. Discover its remarkable influence over your personal and professional interactions as you unlock its transformative power. Brace yourself to cultivate enduring relationships that have the potential to change your life profoundly.

CHAPTER 1:

SECRETS OF THE SILENT LANGUAGE

> *"The way we communicate with others and with ourselves ultimately determines the quality of our lives." (Tony Robbins, 1960, Entrepreneur, Author, and Motivational Speaker)*

WE LIVE IN A WORLD WHERE PEOPLE SAY ONE THING AND MEAN ANOTHER. Getting to the root of what people mean will require more than just listening to the spoken words. People are generally predictable if we know how to read them. That is why developing the skills to hear what is said and unsaid is vital for analyzing the people we interact with daily, whether in a social or professional setting.

We must improve our verbal and non-verbal communication skills to improve our business and social lives. Listening to someone speak and understand what they mean is much easier. Decoding body language is tricky because they are not 100% straightforward. And as a matter of fact, some can successfully hide their body language and make it even more challenging to know their intent.

Nevertheless, when you master the art of reading body language, you can tell when someone is trying to hide involuntary nonverbal cues.

One of the first steps in analyzing people is reading between the lines of their words – not to construe it, but to understand and possibly relate with them better. Therefore, if you desire a good working relationship even with the most challenging person in your company, you need to first understand them by studying their body language, knowing what they are not saying, and hearing what they mean instead of what they say.

Some things to look out for when quickly analyzing people are fidgeting, uneasiness, facial expressions, and moods. Ask yourself what their body posture is like. Are they on the edge of their seat? Is the conversation in a conspiratorial or hushed tone? Do they stop talking when someone walks by or steps into the room? These are some of the things and questions that hold the clue to deeper meanings beyond mere words.

In relating with colleagues, bosses, clients, prospects, and customers, you will encounter different nonverbal cues that give a clear insight into the minds of the people you interact with. But if you do not know how to read these nonverbal cues, you are simply dealing with or relating to the superficial part of people. And, of course, your relationship with them will be as shallow as your understanding of them.

Suppose you encounter someone who effortlessly connects with others and successfully conveys their ideas, products, or services. In such instances, they possess a more profound understanding of people than you might realize. You see, it is not merely how well-read you are in your chosen field or how many years of experience you have in your career that makes all the difference. If you want to excel at relating to people and, by extension, improve your quality of job output, good knowledge of how to read people is indispensable.

Now, let's consider a few skills that are essential to master to read and analyze people effectively.

THE 7 STEPS TO READING PEOPLE

One: Make Personal Contact

Technology has made making friends, meeting people, and communicating with others a lot easier. Now, we can connect to people on the other side of the world without stepping out of bed. However, the same technology that has made communication easier has become one of the greatest obstacles to personal contact with the people in our lives.

From family to friends to even business associates, we can send emails, texts, faxes, make calls, or even hold a conference call without physically needing to be in the same location. And with this, we have gradually lost our people-reading skills. Face-to-face communication is quite different from other forms of communication. In face-to-face communication, you can gauge people's reactions, match them with the tone of their voice, and draw an informed conclusion.

For example, if you need a favor from a colleague, you could walk up to them and ask. They may gladly say yes, and you can see from their eyes that they want to help, or they may say yes, but from the look on their face, you can tell it is not convenient for them, or they are unwilling to do it. In short, there are a lot of possible combinations of meanings that can be deduced in face-to-face communication. If you text your friend on your phone, you will only get a response containing only the facts. You miss out on all the other nonverbal cues that could convey a completely different message from their response.

The very first skill to develop is making personal physical contact with people. Liking someone on social media is different from liking them in person. So, get in the habit of knocking on your neighbor's door and having an in-person conversation instead of just conversing over the phone. Learn to walk up to people and compliment them in person instead of just clicking buttons that do the same on social media. Chat up real people instead of chatting them up on the internet.

I recommend actively re-engaging your people-reading abilities as frequently as possible. Your skills will steadily improve through consistent practice, enabling you to decipher individuals more effectively and accurately.

Two: Observe

Understanding people is more complex than reading the words from a book. Words remain constant and require no observation; their meaning remains unchanged. However, a single gesture can hold multiple interpretations regarding people. For instance, a person's smile can indicate a friendly demeanor. Yet, that person could offer another smile that conveys disdain or anger. Despite it being the same individual and the same facial expression, the underlying meaning differs.

For this reason, is why patience is required to read people accurately. It entails observing their words, how the person communicates them, and their tone of voice. Pay attention to subtle cues such as sighs, shifts in weight from one foot to another, or fidgeting in a chair. Notice if they tap their fingers or squint their eyes. All these clues provide valuable insight into their emotions and intentions within a specific context.

You do not need to form an opinion about one particular gesture immediately. All you need to do first is get in contact with people and observe their general behavior. Take the time to form what is known as a baseline for their normal behavior or body language. When you have determined a person's baseline to a fair extent, you can accurately read that individual. And this happens when you notice a deviation from their normal body language.

Three: Open Up

Communication works best when done from both ends. In other words, it is a two-way street. If you want others to open up to you, you must also open up to them. It is only natural that if people feel they can read you to some extent, they too will be willing to let down their guard so you can read them. It is like giving them a glimpse of yourself so that you can get a clearer view of them.

When your goal is to establish rapport truly, it is essential to be forthright about your views. Merely uttering politically correct statements or conforming to expectations will only elicit lukewarm responses. It is crucial to be honest, and genuine. This approach fosters an environment where others feel comfortable being candid with you, leading to more open and meaningful interactions.

Four: Know Exactly What You Want

Identifying your expectations when seeking a person is crucial, as failing to do so may result in long-term disappointment. What kind of business partner or client do you desire? What qualities do you consider essential for an ideal partnership? A clear understanding of your preferences, whether documented or mentally noted, enables you to compare real-life individuals against your criteria, making it easier to assess if they align with your expectations.

Five: Be Objective

Being objective is one of the most challenging skills in reading people. You must adopt an objective perspective to decipher individuals effectively and accurately. Maintaining objectivity becomes even more arduous when you have a vested interest in the people you're reading. For instance, terminating a new employee may not require much contemplation. Still, objectivity becomes elusive when dealing with a long-standing employee who shares a personal relationship with you. Analyzing their behavior, even if it is detrimental to your company, becomes difficult.

There is a tendency for us to be less objective when a decision is important to us. Nevertheless, if your people-reading skills are anywhere near accurate, you have to remain focused on the task at hand.

Learning how to overcome emotional attachments and the fear of making decisions is crucial to maintain objectivity. Doing so lets you stay focused on your goals and make rational judgments based on the available information.

Six: **Start Fresh**

Accurately reading people means you have decided to drop all preconceived notions and prejudices about them. You are ready to start anew to evaluate every sign based on its merit. In other words, you are dropping all prejudices about sex, appearance, race, age, financial status, etc. It is erroneous to form an opinion about an individual based on your predisposition about people with a particular characteristic. That would be mindlessly stereotyping people and not even close to accurately reading them.

Start by recognizing and acknowledging your prejudices and biases, then gradually let go of them one by one. This approach allows you to begin with a clean slate, enabling you to evaluate situations and individuals with a clear and unbiased mind.

Seven: Decide and Take Action

Once you have evaluated or analyzed a person, decide what to do with your evaluation and take action. There is no point in putting in the effort to create a behavior baseline, read body language, juxtapose them with spoken words to know if they are conveying the same message, and after all the analyzing and evaluating, not take any action on the conclusion of the analysis.

If you have judged a person to be reliable, by all means, strengthen your rapport with them. If they are sloppy, dishonest, or cunning, then there is no likely point in maintaining the relationship.

After analyzing people, taking action (no matter how difficult it may appear) is the most sensible thing. Make decisions and act upon your evaluation to advance your career, build stronger relationships, and improve your business relations.

CHAPTER 2:

OBSTACLES TO OPPORTUNITIES: HOW TO PROPERLY CONQUER OBJECTIONS

> *"An objection is not a rejection; it is simply a request for more information." (Bo Bennett, 1972, Businessman)*

OBJECTIONS AND RESISTANCE ARE COMMON OCCURRENCES IN EVERYDAY LIFE, particularly in business. Ignorantly, some salespersons view objections as a terrible thing. But which is worse: having a client say "no thanks" without looking at your offer or listening and raising objections? I bet you will agree with me that outright rejection is worse. When someone objects, all they need is clarification before accepting your offer.

To effectively handle objections or resistance, you must first shift your perception from seeing objection as bad to seeing it as an indication of some underlying concerns or issues which, when resolved, can bring about the result you seek. And even if it does not produce the desired effect with the client that objected, you would have learned how to present your offer with your next client better.

Objections signify that the other person requires more information, wants their doubts cleared, or needs more assurance. Not everyone expresses objections in the same way. Some object or resist openly, others imply it, while others try to hide it. While handling open and implied objections is relatively straightforward, identifying a hidden objection demands a level of expertise and is where a solid understanding of body language becomes crucial.

If you disregard objections or fail to recognize when a prospect is objecting, you will likely be unable to sell your ideas or products to that individual. It is essential to promptly address objections or proactively anticipate and address potential objections before the prospect voices them. Effectively handling objections is critical to successfully closing deals and securing agreements.

In this chapter, we shall look at a few examples of common objections, how to effectively deal with them, and proven techniques to help you handle objections in specific scenarios.

TYPICAL OBJECTIONS AND RESISTANCE

Identifying objections or resistance brings you closer to effectively handling them. Let's explore some of the most common objections you will likely encounter.

Source

It is important to note that this objection should not be perceived as a personal attack on you, although it may be misconstrued that way. Instead, it is a natural tendency for potential buyers to scrutinize the authenticity and credibility of your product or service. Occasionally, they may even express a curiosity to ask you personal questions to understand your background and expertise better.

For example:

"Why should I trust you? I don't know you."

"I have a reliable customer already."

"How come I've not heard about your company until now?"

Need

The objection of "need" typically leans towards rejection, as the prospect states that they do not require your product or service.

For example:

"I have something similar already."
"I don't think I need this."

Features

This objection is a very positive response. You have done an excellent job of pitching or presenting when you notice this. This objection comes in response to aspects of the details of a product or a service you offer. It simply means they are considering your offer but need clarification. For example:

"The technology is a bit outdated."
"The guarantee period is too short."
"Is there no way to make this smaller?"

Time

This objection revolves around the timing of making a purchase or buying into an idea, emphasizing the need for the right moment.

For example:

"I think I need more time to think about this."

"Perhaps I'll have enough money for this by next month."

"Maybe I'll get back to you after consulting with my partners."

Price

Although many prospects may not directly address this common objection, it often remains hidden beneath the surface. However, with deeper exploration and probing, it can be uncovered and managed effectively. Typically, price objections come up in statements like:

"I didn't budget for this."

"I can get it cheaper elsewhere."

"And this does not include the service fee?"

All these may sound like a "no," but they are natural responses you should expect from someone who does not know precisely what you offer. That is why you need to know how to handle these objections and use them as stepping stones to close your deal.

SIX STEPS TO EFFECTIVELY HANDLE OBJECTIONS

Step 1: Listen

The initial step in effectively handling objections involves actively listening to the concerns expressed by the other person. When emphasizing listening, it entails hearing their spoken words and paying close attention to their body language. Interrupting or cutting off your prospect during their objection can disengage them. Instead, give them the space to express their concerns fully. Remember, your objective is not to provide a generic response but to genuinely comprehend their perspective. Once you have grasped their viewpoint, you can explore the most effective approach to help them consider an alternative view.

Step 2: Summarize their Concerns

Once your client or prospect has finished speaking, pausing for a few seconds before formulating your response is critical. During this brief pause, strive to do more than just appear thoughtful – take the time to genuinely consider their objections and determine the most effective approach for addressing them. Next, summarize the key aspects of their concerns. You can initiate this summary by saying, "If I understand correctly, you are expressing that..." and then briefly restate their main points to allow them to confirm or provide further clarification. By summarizing their concerns, you effectively convey to the client that you have actively listened and genuinely paid attention to their perspective.

Step 3: Dig Deeper

After confirming or clarifying a client or prospect's objection, you can encourage them to provide additional details and expand on their concern. Often, individuals may not initially express their primary objection. Using this approach, you can encourage them to delve deeper, uncover additional objections, or raise their primary concern. Take a moment to explore further by posing probing questions such as, "Apart from this concern, are there any other aspects you are not comfortable with?" or "How has this issue posed challenges for you in the past?"

Delving deeper into their needs and concerns showcases to the client or prospect that you authentically prioritize resolving their objections and meeting their specific requirements. Your objective should be to uncover any hidden or significant objections at this stage. Therefore, the more time you dedicate to this phase of handling objections, the greater the likelihood of finding the root cause of their concern.

Step 4: Address the Objection

Now it is time to address the objection directly. Remember that your prospect or client is objecting because they need clarification, more information, or reassurance – basically, they are expressing fear. So, when you address their objections, you are not merely defending your idea or product but also removing their fears and doubts. Instead of a defensive attitude, take a stance of empathy. You connect more with them when you empathize instead of defending.

Concrete evidence can clear doubts and assuage fears in addressing objections. Share real-life stories if you have them. Refer to other customers' positive experiences if you have any. Give current verifiable statistics if you have some. In general, you should give evidence that can be verified independently, preferably online, such as on websites that are not affiliated with yours (if available).

Step 5: Confirm that Objections are Cleared.

Once you have addressed the objection, it is important to ensure that the concern has been resolved. You can do this by asking a direct question such as, "Does this adequately answer your question?" or a similar inquiry. You can proceed to the final step if the prospect confirms their question has been addressed. However, if they indicate any lingering hesitation or uncertainty, it may be necessary to backtrack to a previous step and repeat the process to provide further clarity.

Paying attention to body language can also offer valuable cues. If you detect any signs of hesitation or dissatisfaction, you can acknowledge it by saying, "I sense there may still be some ambiguity. Let's revisit and try to clarify this further."

Step 6: Pick Up Where You Left Off

Once the client or prospect has objected, it is important to return to the point in your presentation or pitch where the objection originated. If it occurred in the middle of your presentation, take a moment to recap what you discussed earlier and smoothly transition the conversation to continue from where you left off. On the other hand, if the objection arises towards the end of your pitch or presentation, it may be appropriate to begin the closing process and move towards finalizing the deal.

TECHNIQUES FOR HANDLING OBJECTIONS

There are several techniques you can adopt when you address objections. Let us consider a few of these techniques.

The Boomerang

Knowing how to use this technique effectively will almost always guarantee a sale or acceptance. It involves turning an objection or an argument around to your advantage.

For example:

> *"I see you do not have the money now, but we could work out a payment plan."*

> *"I totally agree that it is quite expensive, but your company shouldn't be using the cheap and substandard version of this product."*

The Boomerang technique is highly effective as it allows you to align with the client or prospect's viewpoint while redirecting their attention to consider the potential flaws in their perspective. By acknowledging their point of view, you create a sense of agreement but gently guide them to broaden their perspective and consider alternative viewpoints. This technique encourages them to recognize the limitations of their perspective and opens up the possibility of considering other factors or insights.

TIPPING THE BUCKET

In Step 3 of effectively addressing objections, we discussed delving deeper to uncover additional objections. This process can be likened to tipping the bucket of objections, revealing all the concerns and doubts the prospect may have. By exploring these objections, you gain a comprehensive understanding of the specific areas that require clarification. It is common for the prospect's objections to fall into one or two distinct categories, making them easier to handle and resolve.

Here are a few examples of how to "Tip the Bucket" of objections.

> *"What other reason is stopping you from taking action now?"*

> *"It appears you have more questions. Ask away."*

> *"Aside from this, are there more concerns?"*

This technique is effective for several reasons. Firstly, it provides a comprehensive understanding of the prospect's reservations or objections, enabling you to address them more effectively. Secondly, it demonstrates to the prospect that your primary concern is helping them better understand the offer rather than pushing for an immediate acceptance. This approach fosters trust and builds a stronger relationship with the prospect, as they perceive your genuine interest in their needs and concerns.

REFRAMING OBJECTIONS

Reframing objections is a valuable technique that skillfully transforms the perception of a prospect's concerns. By subtly shifting the perspective, you can reframe the objection as a result of miscommunication rather than a genuine objection. This approach enables you to address the concern constructively, fostering better understanding and facilitating a smoother resolution. For example, you can say, "I am sorry I must have led you to understand it wrongly. Let me shine more light on that."

You can also reframe a seemingly insignificant difference as a major difference. For example, you can say, "Indeed, the color is not common. That is what will make you stand out from the crowd."

Reframing objections can also be effectively employed by spinning the objection around, like the Boomerang technique. By skillfully redirecting the objection, you can present it in a different light, challenging the prospect's perspective and highlighting alternative viewpoints. This approach can help shift the focus and encourage a more open-minded exploration of the objection, leading to a more favorable outcome. For example, you can say, "I agree that the house requires some work, but as you said, you want your personal touch to reflect on it, right?"

This method is effective and straightforward: reflecting back on their objection to them makes it challenging for them to dismiss their own viewpoint.

PRE-EMPT THE OBJECTION

Pre-empting objections is a powerful and efficient technique that can significantly streamline objection handling. You maintain a smooth flow in your pitch or presentation by proactively addressing potential concerns before the prospect even has a chance to raise them. This approach involves identifying likely objections in advance and skillfully addressing them, ensuring they do not resurface later on. The key is to portray the objection as stemming from a flawed perspective and then confidently and firmly provide a compelling response. This approach saves time, enhances credibility, and positions you as a proactive problem-solver.

For example:

> *"Many people will think this is expensive at first, but considering the after-sales service and the payment plan, almost anyone can afford this."*

> *"A few people who hadn't thought it through misjudged it to be too modern for their liking without realizing that technology is advancing."*

Pre-empting works because you have effectively shut off the objection before it is raised.

THE CONDITIONAL CLOSE

The Conditional Close technique is a powerful tool in sales. When a prospect or client presents an objection, you can respond promptly by proposing a solution that addresses their concerns on the condition that they meet specific requirements. These requirements may involve reviewing your proposal in detail, committing to a signed agreement, or purchasing. Introducing this conditional statement establishes a sense of reciprocity and motivates the prospect to take the desired action. This approach effectively tackles objections while fostering a mutually beneficial outcome, propelling the sales process toward a successful conclusion.

To make this method effective, you should phrase your condition in this form: "If I … will you…." Structuring your condition as "if I... will you..." is more likely to yield superior outcomes than phrasing it as "Will you... if I..." The reason behind this lies in the rapid processing of our brains. When the words "if I..." are heard, the mind becomes instantly engaged and intrigued by the potential offering, generating a desire to explore further. In contrast, initiating with "Will you..." triggers the brain to swiftly activate a defensive stance, as it is already primed for objections. Starting by requesting an action may hinder their receptiveness and impede their ability to grasp your proposition's value fully.

For example:

> *"If I can help you figure out a way to get the financial means, will you make the purchase today?"*
>
> *"If I phone your partner to come over, will you take a look at the details?"*
>
> *"You said you prefer a blue one. If I can get you one, will you consider buying it now?"*

This technique works so well because it is built on a principle known as the 'exchange principle,' which creates a social agreement that says you are willing to solve a problem for your prospect if they purchase in return.

THE PUSHBACK

I deliberately saved this technique for the end, as I advise using it cautiously. This method entails countering the objection by rejecting it. In other words, when the prospect objects, you respond by objecting to their objection. However, it is crucial to maintain a firm stance without being antagonistic.

You can achieve this by directly addressing their inaccuracies or demonstrating your awareness of their lack of honesty. Alternatively, you can employ indirect methods that effectively discourage further objections from arising.

For example, you could say:

> *"That, sir, is incorrect. This is the cheapest you can actually get for this quality."*

> *"Perhaps you may want to check your figures again?"*

> *"You and I know that you can afford this if you truly want to."*

When a prospect becomes aware that you have recognized their hidden motives or dishonesty, it tends to put them on the defensive, discouraging them from raising additional objections. They may feel compelled to align with your perspective to compensate for their lack of sincerity.

When executed effectively, directly countering their objection can often lead to a sense of surprise or shock, which increases the likelihood of the prospect accepting your viewpoint.

CHAPTER 3:

MASTERING THE ART OF READING

"The most important thing in communication is hearing what isn't said." (Peter F. Drucker, 1909 - 2005, Author and Management Consultant)

EXAMINE YOUR BODY CLOSELY. IT IS ENVELOPED BY A LAYER of skin that enables you to sense your surroundings. Each of your senses—sight, sound, smell, taste, and touch—has a specific function: to perceive and experience the environment around you. This environment includes other individuals and everything that can be perceived through your senses.

Our design revolves around interacting with our environment and its individuals. To establish meaningful connections with others, effectively communicating is essential. Our senses play a crucial role in this process. When we think of communication, sound and the ears, which enable us to comprehend spoken messages, often come to mind. Additionally, many people recognize the importance of reading and writing to enhance effective communication.

Both verbal and written communication are essential aspects of effective communication. However, it is crucial to recognize that communication extends beyond these forms. While the ear is responsible for processing verbal communication and the eyes, coupled with cognitive abilities, facilitate reading written messages, there exists a significant component of human interaction known as nonverbal cues or body language. These cues may be subtle, yet they convey a wealth of information that is not expressed through verbal means alone.

To effectively analyze people, you must develop the necessary skills to read nonverbal cues. The reason for this is simple: humans are good at masking their true feelings behind verbal communication. But not a lot of humans know how to hide their nonverbal communication.

Acquiring a solid understanding of recognizing and interpreting these cues will give you an advantage in establishing deeper connections with others beyond what they consciously choose to disclose. However, it is essential to acknowledge that the practice of interpreting body language is not infallible and does not hold for every individual at all times. Various factors, such as cultural background or personal habits and reactions, may influence one's nonverbal expressions differently. Nevertheless, these widely observed body language patterns or nonverbal cues hold true for many individuals.

Let's dive into the process of understanding cues exhibited by various parts of the body without any unnecessary delay.

READING DIFFERENT PARTS OF THE BODY

Head Movements

Head movements are among the most easily interpretable forms of body language. However, it can be challenging for individuals who need to learn how to decipher this prominent nonverbal cue to understand the meaning conveyed by different head movements.

Picture a salesperson, for example, trying to convince a potential buyer with his sales pitch. The would-be buyer nods hastily, and the salesman continues trying to convince him. The salesman can't read the body language of his disinterested customer and continues wasting his time talking.

Here's another scenario involving the same salesman. He's trying to sell his product to another potential customer. As he gives his usual sales pitch about his product, the would-be customer tilts his head backward, but the ignorant salesman does not try to clarify his statements. Obviously, he cannot read the suspicion in his potential client's body language.

Here are the most common head movements and their meanings.

◇ Quick successive nods are nonverbal cues saying, "That's enough, next!" If the salesman in our first example knew that, he wouldn't have continued wasting his time pushing a rope – that is an effort in futility and will get him nowhere.

◇ A slow nod shows interest in whatever is being said or communicated. So is tilting the head sideways. Look for a slow nod or titled head when presenting a business idea. If you can get your boss or departmental head to nod as you talk or tilt their head sideways slowly, your point is hitting the spot.

◇ During a conversation, if the person listening tilts their head backward, it could mean uncertainty or suspicion. If you notice that, it is your cue to clarify your points. The salesman in our second example would have cashed in on this knowledge to clarify his statements. When you notice your listener's head tilt backward, address your last point again or ask questions to know if they need clarifications. Say things like, "Would you like me to shed more light on that last point?" or something to that effect.

◇ During meetings, when individuals scratch their jaw or neck, it often indicates their disagreement with the current discussion. As the meeting facilitator, it would be beneficial to allow them to express their perspectives and viewpoints.

◇ When you doubt who the head or the major stakeholder is in a meeting, watch in whose direction most of the heads turn. The decision-maker gets the most attention, while the less-significant persons get less attention.

Reading the Face

The human face is a body part that many individuals consciously control to conceal their genuine emotions. Nevertheless, one can still decipher subtle messages by carefully observing and studying the face. Even when overt facial expressions such as frowns, raised eyebrows or jaw drops are concealed, it is possible to read the face by paying attention to the following indicators:

◇ A warm smile on someone's face is a clear indication of happiness. During a conversation, it signifies that the person is enjoying your company or the content of your discussion. A genuine smile can be identified by how it lights up the entire face. Additionally, pay attention to raised eyebrows, as they often accompany a genuine smile as an involuntary reaction.

◇ A fake smile indicates that the person smiling wants to show approval even though they do not necessarily enjoy what is being said. You will know a fake smile from looking at the side of the giver's eyes. There will be no crinkles on the sides of the eyes.

◇ When a person - a subordinate in your office, for example, tells you something about someone or a prevailing situation in the workplace and repeatedly touches their lips with their fingers, that is a sign that they are either lying or not presenting the whole truth.

Eye Contact

Because of the importance of nonverbal cues of the eyes, I have devoted the whole of Chapter Seven to discussing it. However, I'll briefly mention some quick ways you can tell what this window to the soul is telling you.

◇ Avoiding eye contact during a conversation, such as when a wise business person tries to push you into hurriedly making a deal, indicates that they are hiding something.

◇ Eyes looking down may indicate shame, guilt, or submissiveness. When honest employees are guilty of something, they will likely keep their gaze downwards.

◇ When you are talking to someone, a colleague, for example, and they are shooting glances at the door, it indicates they want to leave your presence.

Hand Movements and Gestures

If you intend to build rapport with colleagues, your boss, or customers, you must get your hand out of your pockets.

◇ Hands in the pocket could mean the person is defensive, lacks confidence, and can also suggest the person is lying.

◇ In a meeting or a group setting, when someone keeps pointing to another person unconsciously while they speak, it shows they share some affinity with that person. You can cash in on that if you seek to get more people to support your opinion in the workplace – getting the support of one of the pair is likely to guarantee the support or vote of the other.

◇ When talking with someone and they hold an object between you and them, it is their way of saying they want to block you out. In such cases, do not try to sell them anything (an idea or a product). Your work is to get them to trust you first.

◇ Having palms facing up while talking is a sign of honesty. Such persons are communicating their genuine thoughts. However, if you are a boss, you should realize that honesty, even though a good trait, cannot be the only yardstick for basing your decisions. You should know when an honest view may not be a beneficial view.

Are They in Your Space?

◇ When someone sits close to you, their body language says they like being around you. If you are selling something (a product or an idea) to them, they will likely buy it or make some form of commitment.

◇ When you lean in, sit closer, and stand near someone, and they pull away, that is a sign that they don't share a mutual connection.

The Feet Don't Hide It

While individuals often focus on concealing facial expressions and other body language cues, they may overlook the significance of their feet in conveying messages. Unlike the face, which can be covered, the feet reveal authentic signals that cannot be easily hidden.

◇ Notice the direction where the feet of the person you are talking with are facing. That is where they most likely want to go. So if you present a business idea to someone and their feet face the door, you should round up your presentation.

◇ Feet pointing towards you is an indication that the person is interested in you or what you are saying. Seize the chance to drive home your strong points before they get bored and point their feet away from you.

◇ Locked ankles are a dead giveaway! If you observe this, especially during a one-on-one meeting with an employee, this has nervousness or apprehension written all over it. They may want to avoid a particular co-worker or anyone else walking in during the meeting. It may also be that they are nervous about an unfavorable outcome of the meeting.

Watch the Arms

The positioning of one's arms can communicate a great deal.

◇ When someone adopts the hands' akimbo posture, with hands on the hips and elbows outwards, it signifies authority, power, or dominance. This stance can also be observed when someone places their hands on a table while standing, particularly in a business meeting setting.

◇ Hands crossed over the chest usually means defensiveness or disagreement. If you are talking with your employees or subordinates, for example, and notice this body language, someone is trying to tell you that they disagree with what you are saying.

◇ When someone has their hands crossed over their chest with a warm smile, it usually indicates self-confidence.

Body Mirroring

Performing similar body movements and speech patterns as someone else is called mirroring. Here's an example of a natural form of mirroring. When you look at a person yawning, you likely also yawn.

◇ When someone mirrors your movements, they are likely into you. Change your sitting or standing posture and wait a few seconds to see if they will mirror you.

◇ If you are a woman and you want to build rapport with another woman, mirroring her exact outfit may kill any chances of doing business with you. Women generally don't appreciate mirroring their outfits.

◇ Men, on the other hand, see dressing.

◇ alike as a chance to become good friends. That friendship may become a life-long friendship that can culminate into a business partnership.

◇ Do not mirror negative signals. If you do, chances are the other person will not want to associate with you even though you are mirroring them.

CHAPTER 4:

IDENTIFYING THE FIVE PERSONALITY TYPES

> *"And those who were seen dancing were thought to be insane by those who could not hear the music." (Friedrich Nietzsche, 1844 – 1900, Philosopher)*

PERSONALITY TYPE IS A RATHER BROAD SUBJECT; YOU CAN GET various personality types depending on whom you talk to or what source you consult. Nevertheless, for this book, we shall limit our focus to the four basic personality types and how their traits drive business decisions, either in the capacity of a business owner or an employee.

Understanding that everyone in a business setting is driven or motivated according to their personality type will help you to relate to them from that understanding. A lack of such understanding causes conflict and misunderstanding in the workplace. To accurately analyze the people in a business setting or the workplace, you need to understand what drives them.

Several names have been advanced for the four basic personality types, but their descriptions remain the same. Now, look at the four basic types and what drives their business focus.

THE DOMINANT PERSONALITY TYPE

Also called the choleric personality type, the dominant personality type describes a person who is always objective, focused, and hardworking. They are goal or result-oriented, always looking forward to accomplishing the task and jumping onto the next job. They are natural leaders;

therefore, they have no qualms about taking the lead.

A business owner with a dominant personality type is driven by purpose. They prioritize results over the specific methods used to achieve them. Their attention remains fixed on the company or organization's overarching goals, avoiding unnecessary distractions. Regarding employee relationships, they tend to adopt a matter-of-fact and straightforward approach. A high level of energy characterizes their leadership style. They are not inclined to tolerate excuses for underperformance and may rely on assertiveness or their traits to lead.

An employee who has a dominant personality type is always an ambitious worker. They go the extra mile to ensure they outperform their previous performance or the performance of other employees. They are ladder climbers in a corporate setting. They are set on the next available position to advance their careers. They believe they are qualified to handle whatever task is thrown at them, no matter the difficulty level, and they are resourceful.

Working with a Dominant Personality Type

Recognizing their high regard for assignments and tasks is crucial to effectively collaborating with individuals with a choleric or dominant personality type. Consequently, they may become upset when encountering underperformance or deviations from expected performance. If you find yourself working under a boss with a dominant personality, it is essential to consistently demonstrate your utmost competence and be prepared to assume a substantial workload. Gaining their respect requires projecting an air of confidence and self-assuredness. Any signs of uncertainty may lead to a loss of favor with them. They prefer working alongside winners or individuals who are proactive and positive.

Dominant personality type leaders are quick decision-makers. If you work with one, ensure that you provide them with adequate information for them to reach prompt decisions. Getting them to function as better leaders should be your target if you want to be in their good books.

If you want to make a choleric leader attend a function, make them see that all the leaders will participate.

An employee with the dominant personality type will make a good unit or departmental head. Coordination comes easy for such an employee. Keep them engaged by constantly delegating tasks to them. Motivate them by offering them temporal leadership positions to get the best out of them.

THE EXPRESSIVE PERSONALITY TYPE

The expressive personality type, also known as sanguine, is characterized by extroversion, which makes them naturally inclined towards tasks that involve interacting with people, including strangers. They possess inherent salesmanship qualities, exuding high energy and strong optimism. Fearlessly embracing competition in business, they readily welcome challenges with an open mindset.

As business owners, they are good motivators, and they relate well with their employees. A business relationship for a boss with an expressive personality type is much more personal and long-lasting. They make their employees feel great about taking on any challenge. An expressive leader leads by their inborn ability to be endearing.

An employee with this personality trait will make a good marketing professional. They are good at training others in their area of expertise because of their ability to be expressive.

Working with an Expressive Personality Type

Sanguine individuals are primarily driven by their inclination for enjoyment and fun. This natural predisposition often leads to a lesser emphasis on organization and structure. When managing an employee with this personality type, assigning tasks that involve socializing or are people-oriented is essential, as they tend to excel in these areas. However, excluding them from critical thinking tasks requiring high organizational skills is advisable. Instead, engage them in roles such as marketing or sales, where they can leverage their charm and likability to increase sales and successfully close deals.

Telling an expressive personality type that an event will be fun will likely excite them to be at it. They also make excellent MCs at events because they are usually open in social gatherings.

THE INTROVERT PERSONALITY TYPE

The introvert personality type is often referred to as the melancholic – these are people who are overly concerned with minute details. They are very analytical and thorough. They are hardly driven by whim when making decisions; their decisions are well thought-out and very calculated. They tend to avoid rashly making business decisions. They would rather delay a decision until they get the facts right than hurry into wrong choices. Rationality is far more important to them than jumping into decision-making. The voice of reason always drives them. However, their desire for detail keeps them stuck in analysis paralysis. And they are most often viewed by others as being very pessimistic or even sluggish thinkers.

A leader who has this personality type will not tolerate employees who bend the rules even if they produce results in the long run. Being morally upright and following due process is a vital character trait for this type of boss. These leaders are known to lead by focusing on detailed procedures and company policies.

An employee with an introverted personality type needs a lot of precise instructions. It would be best to spell precisely what you want and how you want it done.

Working with an Introvert Personality Type

A business owner with an introverted or melancholic personality type must be kept abreast of the task's nitty-gritty. They are interested in all the details that inform a decision.

These types of leaders tend to micromanage others. To convince a boss with this personality type, you must provide ample information in your presentations or pitches. Leave no stone unturned when presenting them with any new business idea.

Employees with this personality type need to know that their actions are in keeping with the organization's rules. So, remember to compliment them on their rightness and ability to look at things from several points of view. Acknowledging and praising their ability to consider multiple perspectives is essential, as this is a powerful motivator for introverted individuals. However, if you are delegating a task that requires a relatively quick decision based on scanty details, you should never consider delegating such a task to an introverted personality. They cannot work with insufficient details or afford to be rushed into making quick decisions. A boss who does not understand this will always have a misunderstanding with such employees.

If you are looking for an employee that will enforce company rules and regulations, consider choosing one who has an introverted personality type. They will ensure every other employee in your organization knows and follows the rules.

To get an introverted person to attend a function, make them see that all the information they need will be presented.

THE RELATIONAL PERSONALITY TYPE

The relational or phlegmatic personality type combines both the expressive and introverted personality types. Because they are highly relational, they work best in groups and always look out for the interest of others. They are outwardly expressive but do not want to be rushed into decisions like introverts. They need time to consider the impact of their decisions on others. However, unlike introverts, they focus less on keeping to rules and regulations. They may go to the extent of sacrificing their interests to protect those of others.

A business owner with a relational personality type does their best to avoid conflict among their team. They are easygoing and protect the interest of their workers to the best of their ability. They tend to take the welfare of their workforce very seriously.

Their employees often perceive them as leaders rather than bosses. These types lead best by forming alliances.

An employee with this type of personality flows well with a group. They are good team players who will hardly verbalize their frustrations so as not to create conflict in a team.

Working with a Relational Personality Type

To get a leader with the relational personality type to agree to any business policy, you must convince them that it serves the interests of all involved. Other people's opinions are of great importance to them, so when you present a business idea, you should ensure that you level the playing field to protect the interest of all involved.

If you are looking for an employee who will be a good follower, seek a relational personality type. Putting them in charge of a team or a unit may not bring out the best in them. They will try to please everyone at best and fail to meet the company's target.

HOW TO EFFECTIVELY MANAGE DIFFERENT PERSONALITIES IN A BUSINESS SETTING

Briefly, let us look at five steps to manage these different personality types in a business setting effectively. This section is designed for those who manage other employees.

Step One – Determine their Type

The first step in effectively managing employees of different personality types is determining their personality type. Are they thinkers or feelers? While thinkers make decisions from facts and logic, feelers depend largely on relationships rather than objectivity.

Observing how each employee handles disagreements and conflicts will give you a clue as to whether they are thinkers or feelers. We shall take a deeper look at this in the next chapter. When you have determined their personality types, you can adjust your management style for each individual. For feelers, try to be sensitive while dealing with them. And thinkers focus more on facts and logic.

Step Two – Establish a Relationship

Certain employees can pose challenges for both management and colleagues. However, investing the effort to recognize their unique personality traits can significantly facilitate the establishment of trust and forge enduring relationships. Ultimately, this will cultivate unwavering loyalty and undoubtedly enhance productivity within the workplace.

Step Three – Raise the Bar

You must raise the bar for your employees if you want more productivity. Standardized work may become tedious, especially for employees who detest working under strict supervision. Raising the bar and allowing creativity to come to the fore will push them to bring out their best. Key into their personality and use it for the greater good of your organization.

Step Four – Determine their Preferences

Check to see what best suits each personality work preference and tailor your developmental programs to follow those preferences. For example, some work better with regular or instant feedback instead of an annual review. Some may prefer a strict set of rules within which they will operate, while others may prefer the freedom and flexibility to think out of the box.

Step Five – Don't Take It Personally

Realize that only some employees like the idea of a hierarchy. Many of them may not be particular about you as a person; it is just in their trait to be reluctant to take orders. Keep this in mind, and don't take things too personally. As a leader who has devoted the time to read, identify, and analyze your employees' personality types, you are more equipped to win their trust, and that should account for some positive change in their attitude towards being led.

CHAPTER 5:

ADVANCED HUMAN PSYCHOLOGY

> *"Once you understand yourself, you can stop fighting your natural tendencies and plan for them instead." (Anne Bogel, Reader, Writer, and Podcaster)*

IN THIS CHAPTER, WE WILL QUICKLY FOCUS ON determining an individual's personality type by delving deeper into their psychology. This step is necessary to establish meaningful relationships with others in a professional or social setting.

HOW TO READ AND DETERMINE PEOPLE'S PERSONALITY TYPE

The renowned psychologist Carl G. Jung popularized the concept of personality types. According to his model, individuals are generally classified into two broad dimensions, which two opposing factors can represent:

1. Sensing (S) as against Intuition (N)
2. Thinking (T) as against Feeling (F)

These four basic personality types are formed by combining these factors: ST (Sensing and Thinking types), NT (Intuition and Thinking types), SF (Sensing and Feeling types), and NF (Intuition and Feeling types).

Note: The letter 'N' represents Intuition instead of 'I' to avoid confusion with another trait we will discuss later, denoted by 'I.'

Determining the Sensing (S) and Intuition (N) Types

You can use the following descriptions below to determine if someone falls into the Sensing or Intuition category.

A person who is a Sensing (S) type is usually:

◇ Very practical
◇ Depends on specific details such as facts and figures to make decisions.
◇ Focused on the present or current problem and challenge at hand.
◇

A person who is an Intuition (N) type is usually:

◇ Highly inspirational and has good insights.
◇ Depends on trends, theories, and insights for decision making.
◇ Focused and concerned about the future.

Determining the Thinking (T) and Feeling (F) Types

You can use the following descriptions below to determine if someone falls into the Thinking or Feeling category.

A person who is a Thinking (T) type is usually:

◇ Very rational, controlled by reason.

◇ Depends on an objective approach and logical analysis to make decisions and solve problems.

◇ Cold, objective, and impersonal.

A person who is a Feeling (F) type is usually:

◇ Very emotional, controlled by feelings.

◇ Depends on values such as good and bad and instinct to make decisions and solve problems.

◇ Warm, sympathetic, and supportive of others.

COMBINING THE TWO DIMENSIONS

When you have identified the individual characteristics of a person, you can then accurately categorize them as Sensing and Thinking types, Intuition, and Thinking types, Sensing and Feeling types, or Intuition and Feeling types.

Note that a person may not display the complete characteristics associated with their type. However, to accurately place them, you should look at which category best describes them to a large extent.

EXTROVERSION AND INTROVERSION

Another dichotomy exists within the previously mentioned dimensions: Extroversion (E) and Introversion (I). When this additional layer of categorization is included, it results in a more nuanced version of the personality types.

Extroversion refers to the inclination and engagement with external factors, such as people and things beyond oneself. An extroverted individual draws motivation from the outside world. Typically, extroverts maintain social connections irrespective of their job requirements. They derive enjoyment from participating in activities and engaging in conversations with others.

On the contrary, introversion is characterized by self-reflection and limited interest in external interactions and the surrounding world. Introverted individual draws motivation from their inner world. Even if their job necessitates frequent interaction with others, introverts typically prefer minimal contact. They often seek solitude to contemplate their preferences and emotions.

Determining the Extroverted (E) Type

Use the following descriptions to determine if a person is an extrovert.

◇ Their energy, drive, and motivation come from external sources.

◇ They initiate or respond to events in the outside world.

◇ They enjoy having numerous contacts with people.

◇ They enjoy talking and expressing themselves in groups.

◇ They do not mind interruptions or others getting into their space.

Determining the Introverted (I) Type

Use the following descriptions to determine if a person is an introvert.

◇ Their energy, drive, and motivation come from within.

◇ They are focused on and think deeply about the inner world.

◇ They prefer to avoid numerous contacts with people unless it is very necessary.

◇ They prefer a one-on-one conversation.

◇ They do not like interruptions and like to have their space to themselves.

COMBINING IT ALL

Combining all the characteristics from the Sensing-Intuition and Thinking-Feeling dimensions and the Extroversion-Introversion dimension will further split the four basic personality types into a more nuanced eight personality types. Hence, our earlier four basic personality types will now become:

1. Extroverted, Sensing, and Thinking types (EST)
2. Extroverted, Intuition, and Thinking types (ENT)
3. Extroverted, Sensing, and Feeling types (ESF)
4. Extroverted, Intuition, and Feeling types (ENF)
5. Introverted, Sensing, and Thinking types (IST)
6. Introverted, Intuition, and Thinking types (INT)
7. Introverted, Sensing, and Feeling types (ISF)
8. Introverted, Intuition, and Feeling types (INF)

CHAPTER 6:

OVERCOME COMMUNICATION BARRIERS BY READING BASIC BODY LANGUAGE

"What you do speaks so loud that I cannot hear what you say" (Ralph Waldo Emerson, 1803 – 1888, American Essayist)

BODY LANGUAGE ENCOMPASSES NONVERBAL CUES AND SIGNALS that are integral to our communication. Experts assert that it plays a significant role in our everyday interactions. Grasping and effectively utilizing body language can significantly contribute to your success in any endeavor.

Whether you aim to finalize a sales deal, engage in business transactions, excel in an interview, spend time with friends, or nurture a romantic relationship, the body language displayed by all individuals involved conveys a wealth of information. Research indicates that it constitutes over 60% of the communication process. Keeping this in mind, acquiring the skill of understanding body language is crucial.

Facial expressions, eye movements, lip shapes, and posture — all these elements contribute to the vast amount of information conveyed through body language, providing insights into a person's thoughts and feelings, and is precisely why body language can significantly assist salespeople in securing multiple sales and impressing potential clients. Additionally, it enables interviewers to gain valuable insights into candidates, helping to evaluate their spoken words and unspoken messages conveyed through body language.

Paying attention and effectively decoding body language can help your career's success. A sales associate, for instance, should be able to decipher clearly what the prospect is saying with the body, the same way he hears the words.

An interview panel should also be able to pick clues and information from an applicant's body language. He should be able to select answers to some questions by carefully analyzing the candidate's body language, even before hearing the candidate speak. Humans generally hardly pay attention and do not react to body language.

Seeing someone smile, for instance, indicates that the person is happy and has received you warmly. The correct response in this scenario is to return the smile.

How to read Non-Verbal Body Language When Doing Business, Making a Sale, or in an Interview

Exceptional salespeople and business professionals have mastered the art of attentiveness and interpreting their prospects' body language. They can capitalize on even the subtlest cues that often go unnoticed by others, using them to adapt their strategies for favorable outcomes consciously.

The best part is that understanding body language is an effortless endeavor. It is a skill that can be learned and, with practice, mastered to help you become an expert in the field. This section of the book will examine crucial indicators that require focus and understanding. Regardless of the area of life, you find yourself in. It is sure to provide valuable assistance.

The Eyes

They say that eyes are the windows to the soul, which holds true as a simple gaze into someone's eyes can unveil a wealth of information, providing insights into their thoughts and emotions.

Whether you are interviewing a candidate or engaging with a prospect, their eyes can communicate crucial information. Humans have limited control over their pupils, making them one of the few body parts that cannot be consciously manipulated.

Let's take a moment to consider this, although I wouldn't be surprised if you already have an unconscious awareness of it.

In certain situations, such as when attempting to close a sale, if your prospect is actively engaged with you and maintaining focus, they listen attentively to your words. Conversely, if their attention is directed towards your goods or products, they are contemplating their potential interest in them.

For example, if you notice some audience members examining your paperwork during a sales presentation, it could indicate that they have a question or require clarification. On the other hand, if someone consistently gazes at the door, it might be a sign that they are eager for the business meeting to conclude. A straightforward approach to generate more interest is to allow them to participate actively. Encourage them to ask questions and voice their concerns.

Remember that when you have a prospect, it's highly likely that they will not directly focus on what is preoccupying their thoughts. It's normal for their eyes to wander around the room. However, in the end, their gaze will inevitably return to the very thing occupying their mind.

During a one-on-one meeting, if you notice a prospect staring down at you, it could indicate that they have something to say but are hesitant to interrupt. Take a moment to pause and create space for them to voice their concerns.

Maintain a relaxed and composed demeanor throughout the entire interaction with the client. Employ a soft sell approach to help the client feel empowered and in control. Keep in mind that excessive staring is not ideal. If your prospects maintain approximately 80% eye contact with you, it may be considered too high and can make them uncomfortable.

Strive for an eye contact range of approximately 60 to 70%.

Pupil dilation indicates that your client is fully engaged and intensely focused, which can be particularly advantageous when reviewing contracts or resumes. Moreover, it has been widely acknowledged that when pupils dilate, it signifies the person's contentment with the information they are absorbing. Conversely, narrowed pupils may indicate distress, confusion, or underlying concerns.

When you see that your prospect's pupils suddenly become narrow, ask about their concerns. Or, better still, take that as a cue to focus and expound on the point that triggered this. While being interviewed, a candidate can also use this information to study the interviewer's reaction to help him gain the upper hand.

Watch for Facial Cues

Humans possess an inherent capacity to utilize their facial expressions to communicate. Even infants and toddlers can convey their emotions through smiles or frowns. Facial expression is one of the earliest forms of communication that babies learn.

It is important to note that humans have a vast repertoire of emotions and thoughts that can be consciously expressed through facial expressions.

Additionally, there are numerous emotions and messages that we convey unconsciously through our facial expressions as well.

For example, if your interviewer consistently displays a smile and nods, it is a positive indication. This principle also applies to business negotiations when closing a deal. You can anticipate a smooth and favorable outcome if your client or interviewer engages in either or both behaviors.

Similarly, if there is noticeable tension in either the face or neck of your client or interviewer, it may indicate unhappiness, suspicion, or underlying concerns. This tension can manifest as a crinkling of the nose, pursing of the lips, and other facial expressions.

Encouraging your prospects to express their thoughts and concerns actively is essential. Your objective should be to address their specific concerns; with them voicing them, it becomes easier to do so effectively.

Learn to Decode the Gestures

Remember that if your client's or interviewer's arm position appears open, it indicates receptiveness to the conversation or process. Pay attention to natural and welcoming gestures that align with the interaction flow. Therefore, if your prospect or interviewer frequently reaches out to you and employs expressive hand gestures, it signifies their openness and is a positive sign.

On the other hand, be observant of folded arms, a tight grip on the arms or wrists, and clenched fists. These are typically indicative of discontent or unease.

During the business process, whether business negotiation or interview, pay attention to the hands and arms. They are one of the best ways to reveal emotions. For instance, during a business conversation you are having, the hands of the other person might rest comfortably on the table. If suddenly, during the interaction, they pull their hands under the table, it might indicate that something went wrong.

Remember, someone making sincere disclosure will usually gesticulate or show their hands!

Pay Attention to the Shoulders and Torso

The shoulder and torso are also vital components in decoding nonverbal communication. As a rule, if your clients, customers, or interviewers like and agree with you, they will tend to lean toward you or come closer to you. On the other hand, there is a significant tendency for them to create space between both of you if you say something unsettling or they disagree with you.

Keeping the factors mentioned above in mind, individuals who turn their shoulders and torso away from you are typically indicating a lack of interest in building a connection. This physical gesture signifies disengagement from the conversation, irrespective of the content. When someone is genuinely interested and engaged, their torso will directly face you. However, as soon as discomfort arises, they may physically turn away, metaphorically giving you 'the cold shoulder.'

Additionally, if someone uses objects like a briefcase, purse, or book to shield their torso, it suggests a defensive stance.

Ensure that you keenly observe these cues without revealing your awareness. We have all instinctively interpreted body language to some extent, even without conscious awareness. However, analyzing the signals you observe and utilizing them to your advantage is crucial.

NONVERBAL COMMUNICATION CUES TO IMPROVE BUSINESS SUCCESS

Nonverbal communication involves using body language to get what you want. People have used nonverbal communication over the years. The previous section has analyzed how to recognize and decode various body languages to help achieve success in whatever endeavor you are in.

This section will emphasize the importance of conveying the right message through your body language, ultimately setting you up for success in any professional endeavor. Whether you aim to secure a deal, present an election manifesto, persuade a client to invest in your idea or attend a job interview, utilizing these body language techniques will empower you to achieve your desired outcomes.

Walk the talk

You do not have to be in a conversation setting to pass the right message with your body language. Even while walking, be mindful of the way you carry yourself. Walk with your head straight, high, and erect. Walk with your chin raised, looking straight ahead.

Learn to walk with strength and confidence. Avoid shuffling along and, instead, pick up the pace. Walk fast like you have places to go and people to see. Your walking style makes people perceive you as active, busy, competent, and confident.

Give a Full and Firm handshake.

For example, when meeting individuals, whether they are clients or interviewers, offering a complete, firm, and confident handshake is essential. This gesture plays a significant role in creating a first impression, ultimately determining your success or failure in that interaction. Handshakes convey nonverbal communication cues that can leave a lasting impact.

For instance, in shaking hands, people can judge your character. Many have associated a firm and robust handshake with the right attitude. Hence, they assume that you are offering excellent service to them.

On the other hand, weak, half, or indifferent handshakes (or even offering the fingers) don't give a good impression about you. It could pass you off as unconfident.

Make a Good First Impression

When meeting a client or interviewer for the first time, extending your hand, maintaining direct eye contact, and greeting them with a warm smile is essential. A simple greeting such as "Hello" or "How are you?" can significantly impact the first impression you create. Attention to these details is crucial as it sets the stage for a potentially successful business relationship.

Sit Erect, Facing Forward

Caring about our body language in business and formal settings is essential. For instance, avoid leaning against the back of the chair during an interview or before a client. Instead, face the interviewer or prospect directly. You do not want to look extraordinarily relaxed and lazy about the interaction. You should sit with your back erect and lean slightly forward. Be alert and present throughout the engagement.

The body language of the person we are interacting with can influence us a lot. You make your client or interviewers interested in what you have to say when you sit straight and lean forward. You get the other party interested in what you have to offer the client rather than putting up a relaxed posture.

This posture unconsciously passes the message that you are on a mission with an important message to convey. With this, the other party will pay attention to you, as opposed to when you are leaning back and feeling relaxed during the interaction.

Get the Other Party to Open Up

In a business conversation, interview, or when trying to make a sale, you should aim for the other party to open up. An understanding of nonverbal communication cues will be of great help in getting insight into their state of mind. For instance, you don't need a soothsayer to tell you that it is not a good sign if the other party is sitting with either hand folded or legs crossed.

A person sitting with a closed hand automatically closes his mind to all you have to say. Folded arms are the body's way of unconsciously blocking out incoming data. An unfolded arm, on the other hand, means precisely the opposite.

Once you observe this behavior, your goal should be to encourage your target to become more open and receptive. A simple and effective way to achieve this is by asking questions. However, if that approach doesn't seem to relax them and their arms remain folded, you can physically hand them something, such as a brochure. This tactic can help them become more receptive to your message and increase their interest in what you say.

Employ Positive Body Language

A crossed leg is a non-verbal signal indicating that someone is withholding information. It can be observed when someone crosses their legs at the feet or ankles, conveying the same message.

In a business setting, remember that your client will likely want to mimic your body language. Hence, be sure you make optimum use of this body language to win over your client. Avoid folding your hands and crossing your feet. Your prospect might mimic this, which will affect the purpose of the engagement.

Ensure you nod, smile, pay close attention, and maintain an upright posture with a straight back. There is a high probability that your audience or client will mirror your body language.

Consider the significant impact these tactics can have on your success in any endeavor. It is remarkable how effectively employing them can help you close deals effortlessly. While it may not come naturally, through consistent practice, persistence, and the passage of time, you can deliberately develop your nonverbal communication skills and harness their power to your advantage.

CHAPTER 7:

THE #1 TOOL FOR EFFECTIVE COMMUNICATION

"To build your self-image, you need to join the smile, firm handshake, and compliment club." (Zig Ziglar, 1926 – 2012, Author, Salesman, and Motivational Speaker)

REMEMBER HOW WE TALKED ABOUT NON-VERBAL CUES IN CHAPTER 3? A handshake is one of the first non-verbal cues that reveal a lot about the personality of a person we meet for the first time. It is body language that announces who you are. Even with its significance as a clue into a person's personality, most individuals still need to be trained in the art of giving a proper handshake that exudes strength, confidence, and assurance.

Consider this: we receive training on dressing appropriately to make a positive impression, deliver speeches effectively, and choose our words wisely when speaking. However, we often receive little to no training on one of the earliest forms of physical contact we have with others, which is crucial in creating a favorable first impression.

WHY IS A HANDSHAKE SO IMPORTANT?

The handshake originated as a friendly gesture to convey that one was unarmed and without weapons when encountering a stranger. More recently, science has shown that "a handshake preceding social interaction enhanced the positive impact of approach and diminished the negative impact of avoidance behavior on the evaluation of social interaction" (Beckman Institute for Advanced Science and Technology, 2012, n.p.).

In today's world, the significance of a handshake extends far beyond a simple greeting to demonstrate friendliness. Your handshake serves as a powerful indicator of your character and sets expectations for others. It creates a lasting first impression about you, especially in business. If you are thinking of closing a deal, landing a job, making a memorable first impression on a client, or getting a subordinate to know you are in charge, you must perfect your handshake.

Equally, as someone who wants to successfully analyze people to see if they are worth doing business with, worth employing, or worth trusting, you must begin to see your hand – your right hand in particular – as an instrument for sizing up or assessing the overall personality of the people with whom you interact.

Mastering the art of a handshake enables you to project a confident and professional image and empowers you to take control of your overall professional presence. You can choose what message to pass across by simply changing the type of handshake you deliver for different occasions. And yes, there are handshakes that suit different settings, such as business, political, religious, or social settings (you do not want to give a fist bump in a job interview, would you?). There is a time and place for different types of handshakes; knowing and using this gives you the advantage of being readily accepted in various settings.

No matter how well you have prepared for a situation, giving a poor handshake or the wrong type of handshake for any given situation or social setting may be your greatest undoing.

As simple and brief as a handshake is (usually between 3 to 6 seconds), it sets the tone for future dealings with the people you meet in both a business setting and social gathering, especially if you are meeting them for the first time. In sales, a simple handshake can make or break a long-sought-after deal. A simple handshake can equally change your entire career positively or negatively.

The point here is simple: a handshake, when done correctly, can open up doors for long-lasting business, career, sales, etc., but when done poorly, it can shut the doors of so many promising opportunities.

Additionally, the simple and brief gesture of a handshake can demonstrate respect and be a way to initiate physical contact in a way that doesn't appear intrusive.

TYPES OF HANDSHAKES AND WHAT THEY SAY ABOUT YOU

There are several types of handshakes and quite a few modifications of them. I shall list a few and briefly show you what they mean. Note that the names I used in referring to these handshakes may differ slightly from the names you may know them by. And as a matter of fact, several names have evolved over time for the same types of handshakes. But it does not matter what you call them. What matters is, knowing how they are done and what they convey about you.

Dead Fish

The limp fish handshake, the weakest grip, is the most undesirable type. This type of handshake has no vigor, no squeeze, and no energy at all. It feels as if you are holding a lifeless, cold fish in your hands. Only give this type of handshake if you want the other person to disconnect from both your hand and anything to do with you. The Dead Fish handshake is a deal-breaker, a career buster, and should be avoided.

This handshake says that the giver has low self-esteem or is indifferent. It indicates that the giver has a passive or reserved personality. If you give this type of handshake, you are screaming to the receiver at the top of your lungs that you are uninvolved, uncertain, or nervous.

Fingertip

Also referred to as the Queen Fingertips handshake, this gesture involves extending only the fingers during a handshake, resembling how a queen offers her hand to her subjects. It is often observed among women. The underlying message conveyed by this type of handshake is a preference for personal space, either due to insecurity or a desire to maintain distance from others. Unless you hold royal status or genuinely harbor negative feelings towards the recipient, avoiding this style of handshake is advisable.

The Pusher

Like the Fingertip handshake, the Pusher handshake exhibits a different attitude. While the giver fully engages in the handshake, they extend their arms, intentionally keeping the receiver at a distance. Respecting individuals' emotional and physical boundaries is crucial when encountering this type of handshake, as it signifies the giver's value for personal space and their need to establish a connection.

The Glove

This handshake, often associated with politicians who frequently employ it, involves shaking hands with one hand while using the other hand to cover the receiver's outstretched hand. This gesture signifies a high level of self-confidence or a position of authority. It can also convey sympathy, as seen when ministers utilize this handshake. However, due to the potential for misinterpretation as excessive confidence, it is not suitable for professional or business settings.

Bone Crusher

This type of handshake applies an extra squeeze on the receiver's hand, almost crushing it. It signifies an intimidating personality or an emotional bully. Avoid this handshake by all means if you do not want to come across as aggressive. Ensure that your grip during handshakes does not become too firm because that could be bad for business.

The Dominator

This handshake is commonly known as the Top-Handed Shake. Unlike the usual palm-facing-sideways handshake, the giver's palm faces downward, covering the receiver's hand and remaining on top. It is a gesture that indicates an attempt to assert dominance and may suggest a superiority complex. If you intend to demonstrate superiority, this is the type of handshake to use.

The Controller

In this type of handshake, the giver pulls your hand towards them or guides your hand in a specific direction. This action signifies a controlling personality, indicating that the giver will likely exert dominance over everything and everyone in their space.

Sweaty Palm

A sweaty palm during a handshake says you are nervous or not confident in yourself; it says you are apprehensive and uncomfortable. If your hands naturally tend to be sweaty, or even if you are genuinely nervous, you could mask this by discretely wiping your sweaty palms with a paper towel before a handshake. If you want to close a deal with an important client, do anything to avoid a sweaty palm during the handshake.

The Proper Handshake

Delivering a handshake that effectively conveys the desired message is crucial to project an image of open-mindedness, intelligence, and confidence. This handshake provides a dry, firm handshake with palm-to-palm and web-to-web contact. Keep your thumb up and your fingers straight throughout the handshake, and remember to wear a warm smile as you engage the receiver's hand.

HOW TO GIVE A PROPER HANDSHAKE

So, we have discussed the importance of learning how to deliver a good handshake and the insights it provides into one's owns personality. Now, let us delve into five simple steps to master the art of giving a proper handshake. These steps can be applied when meeting someone for the first time or interacting with friends and colleagues.

◇ Stretch out your right hand with your palms facing sideways and fingers outstretched.

◇ Firmly hold the other person's hand without exerting too much pressure.

◇ Shake their hand once or twice.

◇ Look them in the eye and make sure to smile. It tells them you are completely aware of them, and you appreciate their time.

◇ Show how verbally confident you are by introducing yourself. You could say, "Hi, my name is..." and state your name (or whatever line you wish to use. Remember to keep it short and simple). If you are meeting someone you already know, it goes without saying that you should skip this last step.

When you can effectively combine a good handshake with eye contact and verbal confidence, you will make a great first impression on whomever you meet. They are not likely to forget you.

Although it may seem tricky to remember how to do this properly the first few times, it is not difficult to master. As always, practice brings about perfection, so do not fail to practice. Of course, you should not wait until you meet the next stranger or your next client before you practice. Start with your family, friends, colleagues, roommates, etc. I know it may feel awkward trying to introduce yourself to your kid brother with a handshake, but see it as an opportunity to practice not letting the awkwardness show up in your handshake.

If you tried but failed to deliver the perfect handshake to someone you are meeting for the first time, do not beat yourself up. Have some cards up your sleeve, like a compliment or a question that can easily distract the receiver of your poor handshake. Indeed, you do not get a second chance at making a great first impression, but you still have time to make up for a bad impression.

TIPS FOR GIVING A GOOD HANDSHAKE

◇ Free your hand: Ensure that your hand is free, particularly your right hand, as it is the most utilized hand in handshakes. Avoid holding items that you will need to shift awkwardly to your other hand or search for a place to sit down when it comes time to shake hands. Also, refrain from keeping your hands in your pockets, as this can create an unapproachable impression unless that is your intention.

◇ Knowing when to initiate a handshake can take time and effort. It can be perceived as taking charge or being proactive, but it may be considered rude in some settings. Understanding the specific situation or cultural norms is important before initiating a handshake.

◇ Handshakes provide valuable insights into a person's character as they involve a degree of personal interaction. Physical contact allows you to understand the other person more deeply. Therefore, avoiding cupping your palms or bending your fingers is essential. Instead, gently enclose your fingers around the other person's hand, enabling you to perceive their unspoken message through touch.

◇ Use your elbows: Let the movement of your hand come from your elbows, not your wrist. With a firm grip on the other person's hand and thumbs locked, shake their hand about 2 to 3 times before releasing.

◇ Convey your message with your eyes: A touch of hands without meeting the eyes is an incomplete handshake. The eyes, they say, are the window to the soul. There are lots of unspoken words conveyed through eye-to-eye contact. Ensure your eyes meet the other person's eyes to convey your passion, respect, power, or self-confidence.

◇ Unexpected handshakes can catch you off guard, leaving the other person in control of the situation. However, there is a way to regain control by using the glove handshake. When someone extends their hand unexpectedly, you can counter their momentum by offering a glove handshake. This unexpected move will disrupt their initial intention and give you the upper hand in the handshake exchange.

◇ Pay attention to the direction of your palms during a handshake. There are instances where your palms should face upwards, while in other situations, they should be sideways. For example, when you are seated, and the other person is standing, extending your hand with your palms facing upwards can be a strategic move. This approach is useful when determining if the other person will reciprocate the handshake. However, it is important to use this technique sparingly, as it allows the other person to take charge of the handshake. On the other hand, when both of you are standing, make sure your outstretched hand faces sideways and maintain a firm grip when shaking hands.

◇ Be mindful of your body language: Your handshake posture also matters. If you are standing during the handshake, lean in just a little bit with both feet firmly planted and face them. If the handshake takes longer than usual, you can step back a bit to make them break the hold. If seated, ensure your back is erect as you stretch your hands for the handshake. Do not bend over or bow except if the setting calls for it (such as greeting royalties).

◇ Informal handshakes: Handshakes such as the fist bump or any secret handshake may not be entirely suitable for persons with whom you are unfamiliar. For buddies and colleagues, it may be appropriate, especially if you are aiming for extra effect. Using a fist bump or giving a dap in a formal setting or for strangers may cause them to perceive you in a light that is not good for your professional image.

◇ Avoid these: Do not pat the other person on the shoulder unless you are their superior (as in boss, employer, or minister) or you are in a position to convey care or sympathy (perhaps to show support or empathy for a loss). Also, give the other person room to shake your hand. Do not hold their hand in a clasp and yank it before releasing. The other person will have no option but to follow your hand movements without enjoying the brief contact.

CHAPTER 8:

THE POWER OF EYE SIGNALS: YOUR HIDDEN SUPERPOWER

"I like getting to the meat of things. You can't get it in a five-minute interview. I like to hone a person. I like to make eye contact." (Larry King, 1933, Entertainer, TV & Radio Host)

TO EFFECTIVELY UNDERSTAND, ANALYZE, AND INTERACT WITH PEOPLE, shifting your perspective from viewing them as annoyances or obstacles is essential. The eyes of the individuals you encounter daily convey various emotions that reveal a unique story.

Something about the eyes says a lot about a person's thoughts in the present moment. The eyes may not readily tell you about a person's overall personality, but it gives you clear clues about what they are most likely thinking at that moment. Even infants can read people's thoughts by looking into their eyes and responding appropriately. They can pick up subtle messages from the eyes of parents and adults.

In this chapter, you will learn how to interpret people's emotions and thoughts through eye movements. We will explore the various eye movements and their corresponding meanings. Additionally, we will discuss the importance of making appropriate eye contact in different situations and how to leverage this knowledge effectively.

THINGS TO REMEMBER WHEN INITIATING EYE CONTACT

◇ Maintaining eye contact encourages reciprocal eye contact: People often hesitate to initiate eye contact due to the fear of it not being reciprocated. However, they will likely follow suit by taking the first step and making eye contact, even if they initially look away. If you attempt eye contact two or three times and they continue to avoid it, it is best to respect their preference and refrain from further attempts.

◇ Avoid being creepy: Properly executed eye contact can effectively convey the intended message. However, when it is unwelcome, and you persistently stare, it becomes unsettling. Remember that even if the other person is not directly looking at you, they can perceive when you have your gaze fixed on them as if they were prey.

◇ Switch from one eye to the other: Try to focus on one eye for a bit and then gently move to the other. Be careful not to dart from one eye to the other, as that can be distracting. Moving smoothly from one eye to the other gives the other person a sense that you are paying attention to them. Avoid staring at the bridge of the other person's nose, as it can be misinterpreted as an attempt to manipulate.

◇ Don't be too obvious: Avoid locking eyes for the entire period of a conversation or interaction. It is okay to look away for a bit.

◇ Don't look down when you break your gaze: Always remember to look sideways when you break your stare. Looking down will tell the other person that you are submissive. It may also mean shame or low status.

◇ Start by practicing with familiar people: It might surprise you that you don't maintain eye contact with those closest to you, such as your family. Begin by practicing with your family and friends, then gradually progress to colleagues, and eventually feel comfortable making eye contact with strangers.

COMMON EYE MOVEMENTS AND THEIR MEANINGS

Raised Eyebrows

When raising your eyebrows, they draw attention to the overall facial expression and are generally interpreted as a desire to communicate effectively. Utilize your eyebrows to convey swift non-verbal messages, such as a desire to be understood or to emphasize a point. You can experiment with this technique in front of a mirror. Look into the mirror and say, "Do you understand?" without raising your eyebrow.

Repeat the same phrase in front of the mirror, but raise your eyebrow this time. You will observe that raising your eyebrow adds emphasis to your words.

Darting Eyes

When someone can't keep their eyes still while in your presence, it means they are uncomfortable or feel insecure. Their eyes tell you they would prefer not to talk with you at that moment. If you must portray a confident presence, do not let your eyes dart even in the presence of the most intimidating client, boss, bully, or the opposite sex.

Squinting and Eye-Blocking

When someone squints at you, they likely do not like what you are saying. Squinting is often a sign that the other person is suspicious or skeptical of your words. When someone squints at you, directly addressing their doubts and clarifying your point is important.

When someone blocks or covers their eyes, it indicates their dislike for something they are seeing or hearing at that moment. Excessive blinking or rubbing of the eyes is also considered eye-blocking. This action of covering the eyes is a natural response to repulsion. Children born blind instinctively cover their blind eyes when they receive unpleasant news, showcasing this behavior.

Gazing

A very personal way to communicate with the eyes is by gazing. Depending on the situation, its use can convey intimacy or disagreement. Gazing into the eyes of a beautiful woman or a handsome man usually tells them you like them. On the other hand, gazing or staring straight into your boss' eyes for a few seconds longer than usual conveys disagreement or opposition.

To convey power or authority, employ the power gaze by maintaining a steady gaze within the triangle formed by their eyes and forehead, effectively staring down the other person.

If you aim to show comfort or support, use the social gaze to stare at the other person making sure your gaze goes within the triangle of both eyes and their mouth.

To create a sense of intimacy, employ the intimate gaze. Direct your eye movement from their eyes to their mouth and down to their body. This deliberate focus communicates your intimate thoughts about them. When someone gazes at you this way, their intentions become unmistakably clear.

Glancing Sideways

Glancing sideways can be tricky, so paying extra attention is important to interpret its meaning accurately. When someone furrows their brows while glancing sideways, it indicates uncertainty or a need for additional information. It can also suggest a sense of criticism or suspicion.

Another type of sideways glance that can be easily confused with the previous one is when someone glances sideways with raised eyebrows. This behavior indicates that the person is interested, and in certain situations, it may suggest an intention of intimacy.

The difference between the two is the furrowed brow and the raised eyebrows. Once you get that slight difference, you can tell the two apart.

Looking Down the Nose

When you adopt a condescending gaze, looking down your nose at someone, it sends a clear message of superiority. You can use this to assert your authority and remind an unruly subordinate of your position of power.

Peering Eyes Over Glasses

When someone peers at you from over the lenses of their glasses, it gives the impression that they are intimidating. If you do the peering, you could use one finger to pull down your glasses for more effect. In a business setting, a woman who wears glasses is perceived to be more impressive.

LYING VERSUS REMEMBERING EYE MOVEMENTS

When someone is telling a lie, you can detect it by observing their eyes' direction while speaking. Generally, a person who is lying will look up and then look to their right. It is an eye movement that indicates that they are, at that moment, using their imagination or are simply lying.

On the other hand, when a person looks up and then looks to their left, it typically indicates that they are, at that moment, using their memory. They are trying to recall or remember something.

However, it is important to consider the person's right- or left-handed orientation to interpret their eye movements accurately. This reversal of eye movement occurs because the direction of eye movement is reversed for left-handed individuals.

SUBTLE SEXUAL EYE CLUES FROM THE OPPOSITE SEX

It is essential to consider the possibility of attraction in a business setting, as businesses revolve around social interactions with fellow human beings. Here are a few subtle eye signals that indicate someone's attraction toward you in a professional context. While you can leverage this knowledge, it is crucial to exercise caution and avoid exploiting the opposite sex. This section will limit these clues to just three, as our focus is not on eye signals in courtship or relationships.

The Helpless Look

When a female colleague or client plucks her eyebrows higher up her forehead, it gives them a look of helplessness. This helpless look works like magic on men because the man's brain is cued to secrete hormones to defend or protect a woman when he sees this look.

As a woman, you can use this to your advantage to get your way with men (closing deals, getting a second chance, etc). As a man, you can use this to your advantage and know that the female is simply trying to control your intelligence.

The Come-Hither Look

Women commonly express the "Come Hither" look toward men. It is a subtle and easily overlooked gesture that involves looking upwards and sideways.

If you are a man who knows this look, you can cash in on it and play along to get what you want. As a woman, this eye movement gives you deniability.

It is not too flirty, but it sure passes the same subtle message, especially with an elusive smile.

The Orgasmic Look

When a woman looks at you with a raised eyebrow and lowers her eyelids, it gives her an orgasmic look. This behavior is a bold move from a daring woman. As a man, tread carefully. Unless she is your intimate partner, it is obvious she's trying to manipulate you into a business decision that may not favor you (or your company) in the long run. A woman who is a go-getter who will stop at nothing (morally right or wrong) will usually use this eye movement to be extra persuasive on her male counterparts.

A Word of Caution

Remember that many business settings do not encourage intimate relationships between colleagues. And in some cases, it may not be healthy to have an intimate relationship with clients. Ensure you do not violate any code of conduct when using this knowledge.

USING EYE CONTACT IN DIFFERENT SETTINGS

Eye Contact in Sales and Business Settings

Maintaining eye contact with clients is crucial for successfully closing deals or making sales, as it helps establish rapport. Be attentive when clients express themselves or ask questions while maintaining eye contact. Their eye contact signifies their genuine interest in hearing your perspective. Take advantage of these opportunities to address their concerns, sustaining their gaze for an appropriate duration to foster trust.

When delivering a pitch, it is common to have multiple individuals present in the room. It is important to remember to establish eye contact with the group leader, their associates, and other subordinates. Doing so conveys that you value and acknowledge everyone's presence rather than solely focusing on the leader.

For job interviews, maintain healthy eye contact with the interviewer. Avoiding eye contact during job interviews is a telltale sign of insecurity or lack of confidence. Only some companies will be interested in hiring such a person.

When you are in a situation where you have to give feedback (critical or positive) to a subordinate, avoid sitting in a face-to-face position. It is a feedback session, not an interrogation session. Arrange the sitting position so the other person sits about 45 degrees across from you. This position makes shifting your gaze from the subordinate's eyes to your paperwork effortless.

Eye Contact When Giving a Speech

Maintaining eye contact while delivering a speech portrays confidence, competence, and trustworthiness. It establishes a strong connection with your audience, enabling your message to be received more effectively and warmly.

Try to make actual eye contact even if your audience is very large. Do not follow the advice to look above their heads – you can't fool anyone. You can't make eye contact with everyone in a large audience, but you certainly can make eye contact with a few individuals. And do not pan your head from left to right as if spraying them with some invisible laser. Neither should you be darting your head back and forth between your notes and your audience. The first order of speech-giving you should handle is to memorize your speech or note the major points so that you will only have to occasionally glance at a few major points.

Eye Contact for Complete Strangers

If you must learn how to handle all sorts of people, you should try to learn how to make eye contact with strangers – even those you randomly meet on the street. Firstly, make sure that you do not appear intimidating or threatening. Keep a neutral facial expression with a soft gaze. Secondly, initiate eye contact only when the person is about four paces from you. And finally, briefly look into their eyes, perhaps for long enough to quickly notice their eye color. If they look back at you, offer a brief smile.

Eye Contact to Show Power

Making eye contact when listening to someone speak, regardless of who has a higher status, is a sign of being charismatic. But when you want to display power or authority, it is best to make eye contact when you speak and less eye contact when you listen. Making more eye contact when you speak puts you in a position of being submissive.

You can also hide your eyes to show power. Using dark shades, mirror shades, or sunglasses can effectively mask feedback from your eyes. The one-way eye communication puts you in charge because you can see their eyes and the message it conveys, but they can't see yours. Have you noticed that police officers in dark shades appear intimidating, or people who don't take off their sunglasses when indoors tend to get on others' nerves?

Another way to show power is to stare the other person down. Maintaining a fixed stare in a non-romantic setting shows dominance. Looking away shows submission. Staring someone down strongly influences their psyche, conveying a dominant message. This behavior is frequently observed in sports such as wrestling or boxing.

CHAPTER 9:
THE QUICKEST WAY TO BUILD RAPPORT

> *"Rapport is the ability to enter someone else's world, to make him feel that you understand him, that you have a strong bond." (Tony Robbins, 1960, Entrepreneur, Author, and Motivational Speaker)*

THE TRUTH IS, THERE ARE PEOPLE AROUND YOU WHO SHARE SIMILAR INTERESTS. Still, you need to know how to establish deeper connections with them to overlook the vast array of resources they can offer. That is precisely why I have dedicated this chapter to demonstrating the most efficient method for cultivating solid connections with the individuals you collaborate with within your business.

Rapport refers to a friendly and mutually trusting connection between individuals, characterized by shared interests, understanding, and concern for one another. Acquiring proven techniques for building a solid rapport with your business partners, colleagues, clients, prospects, and customers is essential for enhancing your ability to establish stronger bonds with them.

By following the guidelines outlined in this chapter, you will gain the ability to intentionally evoke strong positive sentiments from the significant individuals in your life. Mutual respect and high regard will be established between you and them, accompanied by coordination and harmony. Implementing the recommendations from this chapter will expedite the process of building rapport with the people who hold importance in your professional life, enabling deeper connections.

Now, let us dive straight into the techniques for building quick rapport. First, we shall discuss the two main ingredients that can quickly improve rapport building, and then we shall also go through six quick tips required for building rapport.

MASTER THESE TO QUICKLY BUILD RAPPORT

Have you ever met someone for the first time and felt they are easy to be with? The reason is simple: something in them reflects part of you. They consciously or unconsciously mirrored your gestures, posture, seating position, tone of voice, expressions, and even body angle. It didn't take long before you began to feel that there was something about the person that you liked. This feeling of affinity occurs because those individuals were mirroring your body language and speech patterns. Mastering these two ingredients accelerates the pace at which individuals build rapport.

You can use body mirroring and speech patterns to influence people to be open with you. For example, a boss may want to create a relaxed atmosphere with an anxious employee by intentionally mirroring the body language of the subordinate. Copying the employee's gestures and posture may make the employee loosen up and feel freer with the boss.

On the other hand, a subordinate can also mirror the body language of their boss to show support or agreement with the boss's opinion.

This mirroring technique is a subtle but powerful way to influence others. They will literally "see" that you understand them completely and make them feel comfortable around you.

Learning how and when to mirror the body language and speech pattern of someone you like will pay off big time. Be careful not to be too obvious, though, because mirroring too conspicuously will annoy and put the individuals off.

Here are the steps you need to learn to master the art and science of mirroring.

Feel Your Connection

The very first step you need to take is to feel your connection. If you are not feeling connected to a person, likely, they are not feeling the connection either.

To feel your connection do all you can to make the other person your center of attention, at least for the period of your interaction or conversation. Deliberately place yourself directly in their view (if possible, in front of them). Frequently maintain eye contact, a nod to demonstrate attentive listening, and gradually transition from surface-level engagement to genuinely connecting with them.

Mimic the Pace

Mimicking how a person speaks, that is, their speech pattern, is an excellent way to create an instant connection. Observe if the other person talks slowly, fast, loudly, or calmly and try to follow suit. If you have the same accent, that is a bonus too! Mirroring speech patterns is less obvious than body movements but has the same powerful effect as body language mirroring.

Look for the Punctuator

Everyone has a punctuator they frequently use to drive home their point. It usually is a body movement such as a hand gesture or a facial movement like raising eyebrows. If you pay close attention to someone, even if you meet them for the first time, you can identify their favorite punctuator.

To show that you are paying attention to them, subtly use their favorite 'punctuator' when showing that you agree with them. You are most likely to connect with them at this point instantly. For example, a person who snaps their fingers to drive home the main point will connect easily with you if you snap your fingers when saying something like, "Ah! I see your point." There are some punctuators you use without saying a single word and still make an instant connection.

Test

The final step is to test the connection to see if it is not a fluke. You can skip this step, though, because it is entirely optional. And if you choose to follow this step, once or twice is enough to test it. Doing a repeated test is capable of ruining everything.

Here's how to test your connection. Make a noticeable body movement unrelated to the conversation and observe if the other person mirrors the action. For example, you can scratch an imaginary itch, interlace your fingers, cross your legs if you are sitting, or tilt your head and watch what happens. If they mirror your movements, you have established a rapid connection with them.

SIX TIPS TO REMEMBER

Prepare for Impact

Everyone has an opinion about someone they are meeting for the first time. Whether we know it or not, we all have a way of sizing someone up or judging someone we meet for the first time. It is a human thing. And that is why first impressions matter a lot.

The first step to building rapport with people is to create a positive impression, especially during the first meeting. Knowing that you will be judged (consciously or unconsciously), it is in your best interest to be at your very best (or close) when you meet people or someone for the first time.

From dressing to cleanliness and to your general mood or energy that you radiate – let people perceive life and vigor from you. It is normal for people to be attracted to those who radiate liveliness and shrink from those who emit doom and gloom. In other words, putting on a long face, a frown, or a disappointed demeanor will only push people away from you. Remember, getting a second chance to make a good first impression is difficult.

Everyone you meet in a professional setting is a potential source of opportunity. Therefore, prepare your mind and your appearance for impact – for a positive first impact. You never know which connection will take your career to the next level.

Remember the Essentials

Having taken the first step to prepare for a positive impact, you should never forget the essentials or basics of human interactions we have discussed in previous chapters.

When you meet with humans like you, give a good handshake and steady eye contact, and let your smile be the icing on the cake. No matter how well-dressed or clean you appear, if your first handshake is poor and you can't look the person you are meeting in the eye, you have just tanked your first impression!

Another essential thing to keep in mind is paying attention. Do not just hear what is said; listen to what is said. And to show you are present and paying attention to what the person is saying, occasionally give a nod. You do not want to overdo it or nod vigorously. That will be considered trying too hard and will send the wrong signal.

Remember that your interactions must not be non-stop conversations. Allow short silence breaks to gather your thoughts before resuming the conversation.

It is not enough to know how to read body language. What you should also be concerned about when meeting people is what is your body language saying. What does your body posture say about you? Are you all over the place? Are you trying too hard to make your acquaintance? Or do you appear calm and collected? Does your posture say you are self-confident without being arrogant? Are you relaxed or tense? Are you wearing a confident smile or a sheepish smile?

Equally, you must be clear and concise when you speak. Do not bombard people unnecessarily with whatever knowledge you presume you have. Moderation in all you do is very vital in building rapport, especially with new people. You do not want others to perceive you as someone desperate or a showoff. Remember to be transparent also. Transparency has a way of drawing like-minded people to you. It is an instant turn-on for many people, just as dishonesty is an instant turn-off.

Keep your verbal and nonverbal communication in top gear to build a strong rapport with people.

Emphasize Similarities or Commonalities

In its basic meaning, rapport refers to a feeling of similarity or commonality. Finding and emphasizing the similarities you share makes you feel you've known each other for a while, even if you just met the same day. A common example would be when you have shared interests, such as enjoying the same sports or pursuing similar hobbies as them. When you talk about what you like and are passionate about, you tend to let down defenses or barriers and allow the other person to come into your life.

It's important to note that sharing a passion for football, for instance, doesn't automatically guarantee to like everything about the other person. It would help if you continued seeking additional commonalities and similarities to establish a strong rapport. As you discover and highlight more shared interests, the connection deepens.

Don't Fake it

One quality that will endear you to people is being yourself. Being honest and genuine makes people quickly develop trust in you. Do have it in mind that you are unique. Therefore, it is pointless to want to be another person. You are looking for people with the same interests as you. If you hide your true self behind a mask, how will those who share your interests recognize and feel drawn to you?

To build a strong rapport with others, you must remember that negative behaviors such as cheating, lying, or backstabbing are a no-no. These behaviors are capable of destroying everything you have built. Avoid them like the plague.

Read Body Language

It is important to perfect your verbal communication first and then ensure that your nonverbal cues synchronize with what your words are saying. If you put in the effort to make your words and body language agree, it will be easy for you to recognize nonverbal cues in others too.

Humans communicate on several levels – words are just one level. The body speaks on a deeper level than mere words. Connecting with people on a deeper level requires a deeper understanding of their nonverbal communication. Reading body language tells you who truly shares your interest, who is faking, who is trying too hard, and who is hiding something.

Throughout this book, I have dropped several clues and tips on effectively reading body language. Take the time to study them to improve your body language reading skills and connect deeply with people.

Empathize

There is a compelling reason why people readily connect with empathetic individuals. It is because most people have an underlying need to be understood. If you can harness this ability, you can forge a remarkably robust connection in the shortest possible timeframe.

You see, we all view the world using different lenses. Our beliefs, fears, environment shape our lenses and so many other indices. This lack of shared perspective makes it easy to pass judgment on others, considering them wrong simply because they don't view things from the same vantage point as we do. Their words and actions are easily termed inappropriate to many, except the few who know how to empathize.

That is to say, if you can place yourself in someone else's shoes and view the world from their unique perspective, you will most certainly not judge them harshly. Gaining the ability to see things from others' perspectives proves challenging for many individuals. Consequently, only a select few who have cultivated this skill can genuinely forge deeper connections with others.

If you empathize, you will not take things personally. You will understand that people's views about you are simply that – their views. It does not reflect who you indeed are. Flip the coin, and the same applies to others. Your personal views about others do not reflect their actual people. They are your views!

The purpose of reading people to form an opinion about them may appear contradictory to this idea. Well, there is no contraction whatsoever. Instead, when you perfect your skills in reading people, you will not only accurately create an informed opinion about them, but it will also help you see their point of view and connect with them on a deeper level. Remember, you are not learning to analyze people because you want to judge them. What you are doing is to understand them to better relate to them.

The Bottom Line

It is simple to build long-lasting rapport if you know how. Nevertheless, building rapport is a manageable task. You can do it. After all, we are all social beings, except that some of us have allowed ourselves to express that social part of ourselves more freely than others. Suppose you want to tap into the abundant resources deposited in the people around you. In that case, you should allow for a stronger connection with those with whom you have identified as having similar views.

Remember, you are not taking undue advantage of the people around you by building rapport with them. By employing these proven techniques, you are enhancing your social circle and benefiting everyone involved in the process.

CHAPTER 10:
ADVANCED BODY LANGUAGE READING

"What you do speaks so loud that I cannot hear what you say" (Ralph Waldo Emerson, 1803 – 1882, Philosopher)

IN CHAPTER 3, WE DELVED INTO THE REALM OF COMMON BODY LANGUAGE and explored its potential interpretations. In this chapter, we shall take that knowledge a step further by looking at some nonverbal cues that are more evasive. If you can identify these cues, you can improve your evaluation and make better decisions.

Remember that I shall be discussing this with particular reference to a professional environment.

The principles remain applicable across various social settings and scenarios. However, note that the context within which an individual expresses any nonverbal cue will ultimately determine the signal's meaning. It is also worth noting that you should not base your evaluation on one single nonverbal expression. Combine two or more body languages in other to get a relatively accurate reading of someone's hidden or nonverbal intentions.

The following are some more subtle body language and their possible meanings.

UNCROSSING ARMS AND LEGS

When presenting an idea or pitching a product, notice if your audience is crossing their arms or legs. If they are, take a short break from your presentation and make them uncross their arms and legs. You can do this by directly asking them, or if it is not appropriate to ask them directly, you could try changing their position or doing something that will make them uncross their arms and legs.

So, what's in the uncrossing of the arms and legs? When arms or legs are uncrossed, it improves memory. Your audience unconsciously blocks you out with crossed arms and legs – it is a defense body language. Uncrossing them will allow more memory retention of what you are listening to.

GLANCING AT THE TIME

When someone glances at the clock or their wristwatch, they convey a message that signifies their urgency to be elsewhere. You must be observant to catch this glance.

When pitching a sale to your prospect or making a presentation to a board of executives, it is imperative to pay close attention to them and notice if they unconsciously tell you to round up your presentation.

You can also use this body language to signal to someone in a meeting that they are taking longer than necessary, especially if the person is your subordinate or employee. Doing this when someone superior has the floor can be seen as being very rude. Avoid it by all means.

THE CHIN JUT AND BATTLE STANCE

These two nonverbal cues are typically infrequent in a professional setting unless there is a significant imperative to meet a deadline or some other compelling form of pressure.

The chin jut usually indicates anger, while the battle stance has a person placing both hands on their hips with their feet widely planted means rage. While this may not resort to a physical fight because of the professional or business setting, it usually is followed by a barrage of verbal exchanges of hurtful words.

When you notice a person going into the battle stance or having a chin jut, it is your cue to quickly change the subject of discussion or avoid them altogether for that moment. Take a break to allow strained nerves to calm down. If you must keep discussing the same issue causing tension, direct the conversation to something reassuring or pacifying.

SMILING

Smiling may seem like common body language, and indeed it is. However, smiles do not always convey the meaning people commonly associate with them.

Smiling has been commonly identified as the body language for friendliness. Nevertheless, smiling less frequently indicates the person is amicable and welcoming. On the contrary, they are unconsciously saying they are weak or submissive.

As an employer, if you observe an employee consistently wearing a smile when conversing or in their presence, it signifies their unwavering loyalty and compliance to you. These types of employees will go the extra mile for you.

As an employee, you can utilize smiling to gain favor with your boss. However, if you wish to avoid creating the perception of weakness, you should significantly decrease the frequency of your smiles.

LEGS AND FEET

As mentioned in Chapter 3, it is difficult for most people to hide their true feelings from showing up on their legs and feet. But I am not just talking about the feet pointing towards you or the door, which may mean the person is interested in you or secretly wishes to leave the meeting or conversation. The feet convey more than that; you need to learn to read advanced body language to ensure you get all the other messages that the legs and feet convey.

When an employee begins to shuffle their legs, especially when seated or wrapping their feet around a piece of furniture or each other, it is a sign that they are under a lot of tension. They are trying to cover up something if it is an interrogation. Increased feet and leg movements signify increased stress and anxiety.

When interrogating someone, it is good practice to make them sit in a position that gives you a clear view of their entire body. This way, you can observe their feet and leg movements more clearly.

LOW TONE

Speaking in a low tone conveys authority, making it ideal for a boss or leader. Pay attention to their tone in a room with multiple people to identify the authority figure. It's important to note that the person with the most resounding voice is not always the boss, as women can also hold leadership roles and have lower tones of voice.

Drop your voice tone to its lowest when you want to show you are in charge. But many people do not know the tactics to keep their tone down. So when they speak, their vocal inflection diminishes the command in their words, even if they hold positions of power.

Here's a quick tip to keep your voice tone low.

Let your voice slow down to its optimal pitch by pressing your lips together and humming or repeatedly making the "um hum, um hum" sound for a few seconds. When you eventually speak up, your voice tone will significantly drop. For females, ensure that your voice drops when you end your sentences.

Keeping your pitch high at the end of your sentences will make it sound like you seek approval even when giving a direct order. Or you will sound like someone asking a question. Try practicing and getting used to the authoritative arc, which means, when stating your opinion or making sentences, your voice should begin on one note, rise in pitch as you are speaking, and finally drop down at the end of your statement.

FACE-TO-FACE

Sitting face-to-face with the speaker in a meeting or presentation unconsciously tells them they have your undivided attention. Even if your sitting position does not allow for a direct face-to-face, you can turn your head and torso towards them.

Checking your phone, multitasking, or seeing how others react may not encourage the speaker. Assuming a face-to-face position also applies in a one-on-one situation. So, if you want the other person to speak up and express their sincere opinions, ensure you are directly sitting facing them.

THE POWER POSE

Standing with legs and arms open is the power pose. It indicates self-confidence. If you are doubtful or unsure and need to boost your confidence, especially when addressing your superiors, assume the power pose for a few minutes, and your confidence level will rise.

The power pose links to the hormone testosterone, which is associated with dominance and power. Additionally, the power pose stimulates the release of testosterone in both males and females. If you find yourself training employees on how to give a presentation that will influence their audience, teaching them the power pose is beneficial.

CHAPTER 11:
THE EASIEST WAY TO BUILD CHARISMA

> *"How can you have charisma? Be more concerned about making others feel good about themselves than you are making them feel good about you." (Author, Dan Reiland)*

Are you running for mayor of your town?

Are you a salesman hoping to close some deals?

Are you a pastor who wants to connect more with your congregation?

Are you an entrepreneur seeking to attract investors?

Do you want to increase your circle of friends?

Are you a parent trying to strengthen the relationship with your child?

CHARISMA IS ONE POTENT TOOL FOR SUCCESS that can help in whatever sphere of life we find ourselves in. Charisma is that quality that makes people like you, attracting people to you naturally and making people want to listen to you. It is an essential trait for leaders who want to get on the right side of their followers.

Developing charisma may appear challenging and mysterious, often considered an innate trait bestowed upon a fortunate few. Nevertheless, the encouraging revelation is that individuals can cultivate charisma. Through unwavering determination, deliberate practice, and wholehearted devotion to the critical facets of enhancing charm, one can metamorphose into an individual who exudes elegance and earns universal adoration.

In pursuing character, this chapter emphasizes three pivotal aspects of developing charisma – presence, power, and warmth. Dedicating to these elements can initiate a transformative journey toward a fulfilling and joyful existence.

FIRST CHARISMA COMPONENT: PRESENCE

Whenever you discuss something with someone and feel you don't have their attention, I bet you feel pretty annoyed. A lot of people are guilty of this. People hardly engage with other people during the interaction.

When you look at this in the light of developing charisma, it means making yourself captivating to other people. No, this is not about tooting your own horn but making others feel good about themselves. In other words, a brief interaction makes the other party feel good about themselves and leaves them feeling better than when you met them.

To create this captivating feeling, you have got to focus your emotional and mental energy on the other party. People love being recognized and acknowledged; it is an inherent human character.

Conveying presence is simple yet could be difficult for some people to achieve; here are some helpful tips for developing it.

Bring Yourself into the Conversation

In other words, practice mindfulness. We have difficulty being in the present because we are not mindful. While we might be interacting with someone, our mind is a mile away, engaged in other things.

A trick to help with this is directing your attention to body sensations, most often the breath. It is not about paying attention to your breath but using it as a trigger to bring you back into the moment.

Be Physically Comfortable

Be sure you are comfortable on the seat and in your clothing. Paying attention will be hard if all that occupies your mind is how uncomfortable you feel. In this regard, choose a comfortable posture. If you engage people in your home, set the thermostat to a comfortable temperature.

Maintain Eye Contact While Talking

Research and studies have confirmed that individuals who make eye contact convey warmth, sincerity, confidence, dominance, honesty, and emotional stability. Besides eye contact making you appealing, it also helps you interact well. With eye contact, you build intimacy, with the other party feeling warm, confident, and connected to you. Be careful, however, not to make the other party uncomfortable with too much eye contact

A Nod to Affirm you are Listening.

In addition to maintaining eye contact, you can utilize head signals to demonstrate your attentive presence. Body language, mainly nodding, serves as a valuable aid. However, you must exercise caution with excessive nodding, as others may perceive it as an overly eager attempt to please them. Undoubtedly, this can have an adverse effect. It is essential to note that effective nodding requires active listening to the person's words and cues.

Ask Clarifying Questions

A simple way to let the other person know you are with them throughout the conversation is to ask clarifying questions. When asking clarifying questions, you should do so when the person has finished talking. For instance, questions like "When you referred to_____, what were you talking about?

You could also rephrase part of what the person said and add, "Am I getting you right?"

That is just a part of the equation. After presence comes power and warmth. Let us get on with the second element of developing Charisma – Power!

SECOND CHARISMA COMPONENT: POWER

When we mean charismatic people are powerful, it doesn't mean they wield massive power; neither are they rulers of empires. Many people often assert that great power lies in humility.

Power:

"*…means being perceived as able to affect the world around us, whether through influence on or authority over others, large amounts of money, expertise, intelligence, sheer physical strength, or high social status.* "according to Cabana.

Increasing your charismatic power comes with practice. It is not something you develop overnight. Here are some ways to boost your charismatic power:

Improve Your Confidence

To harness the power, you must cultivate an internal sense of empowerment. When you achieve this state, you can emanate and share this energy with those around you. Self-assurance and confidence help draw people to you and to be confident. You have to develop your mastery. Whatever field you are in, be an expert, a person of knowledge, or a resourceful person who knows what he is up to. When you attain mastery in your field, you will feel confident, reflecting on how you carry yourself.

Know Something about Everything

Okay, something about everything is an overstatement, but you get the point. The idea is to be vast in many subjects and know a little about many things. Remember that you cannot affect the world around you without intelligence. Besides, the more conversation you can comfortably add and contribute to, the wiser you appear to people.

The simplest way to build this is to read whenever you can!

Be Smart with How You Dress

One of the most influential power cues is clothing. That is why military men and law enforcement agencies wear unique attire, as it demonstrates authority. With a high-status outfit, you can influence others. Remember that this is not entirely about being seen as powerful but also about feeling good about yourself, something you can get from dressing appropriately.

Be sure to take steps every day to dress better. It is not about burning a hole in your pocket to get the latest designer outfits. We are discussing reasonable upgrades to show you are on top of your game.

Assume Power Poses

Some poses, such as the arm akimbo, are believed to convey power, so we often see many superheroes adopting this position as a familiar and favorite power pose.

You can also lean back in your chair and interlock your hands behind your head. You could convey power in a meeting by standing and leaning forward with your hands on the table before you.

Another power pose is lifting your hands in the air before you. Be thoughtful about when you want to use this pose so you do not appear strange.

The beautiful thing about the power pose is that besides making others see you as powerful, you also feel manly. According to research, adopting power poses can help increase testosterone levels and decrease cortisol. Doing so makes you feel more confident and less stressed, which significantly aids in your quest to develop charisma.

Take Control of Your Environment

Familiarity with our surroundings creates a sense of ease and reduces anxiety. As a result, we gain a feeling of control, which enhances our confidence. When it comes to negotiations, companies often engage in intense arguments about the choice of venue, driven by the desire for familiarity. These discussions occur before negotiations, with each party striving to secure a home advantage.

Speak Less and Speak Slowly

Exerting power goes beyond physical presence and involves active conversation engagement. However, it does not entail dominating the discourse. Compelling individuals grasp the significance of conveying concise messages, as it is through brevity that their communication holds weight. Therefore, powerful individuals prioritize listening rather than incessant talking, which captivates the attention of others when they do choose to speak.

Influential people are not bothered by the "awkward" silence; they love it. They space out their conversation with silence. Typically, people are usually desperate to fill the silent gap. Influential people know that the other party will likely give out vital information, a helpful advantage during those periods of anxious chatter. Job interviewers, interrogators, and others resort to silent treatment to reveal the person's vulnerability.

In the chapter on lying, it is important to note that one of the signs of lying is the discomfort with silence. Liars tend to keep talking to fill the silence with claims or explanations.

On a final note, about developing charisma, I will explore the last piece of the puzzle – warmth, for it is only when you can successfully harness the three arms that you will develop charisma.

THIRD CHARISMA COMPONENT: WARMTH

With warmth, people perceive you as caring, gracious, empathetic, and approachable. They are at ease, comfortable, and can be themselves in your presence. Warmth has to deal with the human need to be loved, cared for, and understood. Parents and caregivers have instilled the need for love, care, and understanding in every individual from childhood.

Warmth is a mother packing an umbrella in a child's bag before they go to school. Warmth is a father pecking a child's forehead as he lifts them after returning from school. Although we grow up and fly out of the nest, deep down, we still crave acceptance and care!

Warmth is essential and works perfectly in sync with the other two elements before it can help build charisma. If you have power without warmth, people will see you as arrogant. And if you have warmth without power, people see you as weak and an attention seeker.

In developing warmth, try and adopt the following points.

Practice Gratitude

With gratitude comes the joy of heart. Besides, people who are fond of practicing daily gratitude are happier than others who do not. You have numerous options to incorporate gratitude into your practice. Every day, for instance, list things you are grateful for. As you develop this, you can put your problem in perspective and be more relaxed, which radiates to people around you.

Prioritize Face-to-Face Relationships

A face-to-face connection and interaction with other people trigger empathy in the brain. This explanation refers to the fact that research indicates college students today show less compassion than their counterparts 30 years ago. They prefer communicating and relating with people online rather than through physical interaction. When we don't connect physically, the possibility of being indifferent and exhuming an evil motive exists. Hence, reduce your time on the phone chatting in front of your computer screen and interacting with people offline.

Be Genuinely Interested in Others

To develop warmth, you must show interest in getting to know the other party. Ask clarifying questions that reveal more of their personality. With this, you understand them and know what gets them going. From everyone you interact with, you can learn something about the person and life in general.

Give a Firm Handshake

Touch is also essential in generating warmth in others. Giving a firm handshake is not about flirting and invading others' personal space. The handshake is a good chance to establish skin-to-skin contact and make it firm, warm, and full of life.

Alongside the firm handshake, offer a smile. Offering a smile will keep the other party relaxed and connected with you.

Keep Details, Anniversaries, and Dates in Mind

I have noticed that when people remember my birthday, especially those not close to me, it makes me feel special. And I bet other people think this way as well. Posting generic birthday greetings on someone's Facebook wall is not what we're aiming for. The goal is to stand out from the crowd and make a more meaningful impact.

Send a card, make a call, or craft an email. See this as an opportunity to ask about their well-being as well. In addition to that, keeping details in mind is very important.

Give Thoughtful Gifts

I am not asking you to burn a hole in your pocket to get someone a gift. It does not have to be something big. I am talking about things that let people know you are paying attention to them. Your wife has often come back from work soaked in the rain. Getting her an umbrella is very thoughtful. You can imagine how glad she will be when you mention that you hate seeing her drenched every time.

Smiles, Costs Nothing

With a smile, you not only feel warmth but also convey warmth to others. It is one of the easiest ways to express warmth. Smiling is so powerful that studies have shown that it can instantly make you happy even when unsatisfied. Go ahead and grin. It will pave the way for a warm mindset.

Besides making you happy, smiles make you confident, approachable, and more attractive to others. Also, research revealed that people who smile often are more attractive than others who do not. One thing anthropologists and psychologists have come to agree on is that smiling is a tool that signifies to others that we come in peace or we have good intentions.

I can go on and on about how smiling helps you and contributes to your quest to build charisma. It will cost you nothing. Be sure to train yourself to smile at everyone you meet.

Relax Your Posture

Depending on the circumstance, an erect posture might make you appear cold and stiff in some situations, even though it reveals power and confidence. Hence, if you are trying to create warmth, have a relaxed posture.

Don't stick your chest out and throw your shoulders back. Instead, assume a natural and comfortable position with your back, shoulders, and chest. You want to look approachable, not like a dictator.

Mirror their Body language.

A study confirms that when you copy how someone talks and mirror their body language, you build trust, and they also find you attractive. According to psychologists, mirroring another's body language triggers limbic resonance between the two parties, creating strong feelings between them.

Be careful, however, not to make it too apparent, or you appear as if you are mocking them. If they talk slowly, slow your voice down as well; if they lean back in their chair, lean just a little bit back. Be sure to wait a few seconds before mimicking their position.

There are times when mirroring body language could backfire. You don't want to mirror an angry person's tone or body language. Escalating the whole issue results from mirroring an angry person's expressions or body language.

CONCLUSION: BUILDING CHARISMA

If you have followed this book up to this point, you probably recognize that charisma is not an inherent trait exclusive to a specific group. Instead, individuals can develop charisma over time through patience and practice.

The tools provided above are infallible in helping you build charisma. It, however, only comes on a silver platter as you must practice once the habits become part of you. In time, you can balance the three components, transforming you into a loveable person everyone wants to be around.

Charisma can be used for both good and bad, being a neutral trait. However, be sure to use yours to increase your circle of friends, draw people to you, make people like you, increase your sales, and strengthen your relationships with people altogether. Make sure to actively participate in meaningful endeavors in your professional and social life, as charisma will grant you opportunities inaccessible to those lacking it.

CHAPTER 12:

HOW TO TURN OBJECTIONS INTO OPPORTUNITIES

> *"To build a long-term, successful enterprise, when you don't close a sale, open a relationship." (Patricia Fripp, Author, Speaker, and Sales Presentation Trainer)*

THIS CHAPTER WILL EXPLORE TECHNIQUES FOR IDENTIFYING OBJECTIONS or rejections to your proposals or offers. You can enhance your awareness in such situations by acquiring the ability to interpret subtle signs of rejection, typically understood by experts.

When presenting a business idea, making someone an offer, or pitching a sale, your job is not just to make an excellent presentation. Your job also includes listening to what your audience is not saying. In other words, you are not just talking with your mouth and hearing with your ears; you are also "hearing" with your eyes and your perception, the messages their body language sends. This chapter aims not just to get people to accept your ideas or products but to connect better with them and help them see your point of view.

SIGNS OF OBJECTION

Below are examples of body language that indicate objection or rejection. Watch out for them and tackle them effectively before your audience verbalizes their objections. It will be as if you are reading and analyzing their minds in their heads.

Hands and Arms

Sign language is based entirely on hand and finger movements, meaning the hands can communicate much more than many people realize. In a meeting or a presentation, watch out for the following hands and arm signals that tell you objection is brewing, and then take appropriate steps to address the yet-to-be-verbalized objection.

◇ Your prospect begins to play with objects like a pen: They tell you they are bored. This behavior of playing with things like a pen could also indicate that they are annoyed. In both cases, give them a chance to become part of the conversation by asking them questions requiring them to share their thoughts about what you are offering.

◇ Your client is drumming their fingers: This is one of the most unmistakable signs of impatience. Your client may not be interested in all the details you share with them or doesn't have the time for lengthy presentations. When you notice this body language, skip the nitty-gritty and hit the main points.

◇ They cross their hands or turn their body and hands away from you: These people are telling you they do not like or are not interested in what you are saying. Bring up another subject or find another way of offering the same idea or product. If not, end the interaction and save both of you time and energy.

◇ They are pointing fingers at you or your product: This hand movement says they are trying to intimidate you. Addressing your client's concerns or questions may address the situation.

◇ They are leaning on one arm or resting on an armrest: That person (your employee, boss, or client) wishes to leave the meeting. A great way to quickly tackle this is to give them room to air their views. Note, however, that this body language may be inaccurate; therefore, you should only sometimes conclude by isolating this sign alone.

Feet and Legs

If you cannot figure out exactly what a person's facial expression means, look at their feet. People hardly consciously control their foot and leg language; if they agree with you, the feet will easily reveal it.

◇ When clients wiggle their feet or legs, that's a sign that they are bored. Perhaps you have been doing all the talking, and it is time to involve them in some of the talking.

◇ If your potential buyer, client, or employer is tapping their feet, they likely feel they've got the upper hand, an edge, or an advantage in a negotiation. The tapping of their feet may not seem like the body language of the objection, but it sure tells you that you are not on the winning side.

Eyes

When someone is about to reject or object to your offer or proposal, they cannot hide it in their eyes, as the pupil is one of the few body parts anyone can control.

When analyzing someone's eyes, here are some common signs to look out for:

◇ When a prospect's pupil narrows, it is more than likely that they have serious concerns about what you are presenting. In such a case, you should slow down with your pitch and ask if they need clarification about something you have said.

◇ When someone is staring you down while you are talking, they are concerned about what you say.

If you are selling an idea or product, stop and ask them if they have questions about your offer. If it is your boss, you should politely ask if they have concerns about your ideas. And if it is an employee or a subordinate, you can ask them (if appropriate) to air their views.

◇ When a prospect's eyes return to a particular area/object, your paperwork, for example, may be worried about having to fill out all the required information. You should ask if they are concerned about it and assuage their worries.

◇ When someone keeps glancing at the door while you are talking, their eyes unconsciously tell you they want to leave if you haven't finished your pitch or presentation. Cash-in on this clue and re-engage them by letting them be part of the conversation. However, if you have completed your pitch and there is nothing further to say, wrap up and let them leave. Allowing them to go after concluding the presentation will save all parties valuable time.

Others

Here are additional cues to be mindful of when presenting to a client. Keep an eye out for the following signals as well:

◇ **Pursing of the lips:** Pursing indicates that they are not telling you something. They think about what you are presenting. Perhaps they are being polite not to offend or hurt your feelings, but they will not agree with you. When you see this body language, give them a chance to air their opinion. They may not be forthcoming at first, but with some persuasion, they will tell you what the objection is.

◇ **The crinkle of the nose:** This indicates mild disagreement. When you see this, the prospect has an objection but is still determining if they are right or wrong about it. The objection is still forming, so they may want to hear more before deciding to voice it. Cash in on this mild disagreement gesture and nip it in the bud before it develops into a full-blown objection. Ask them to tell you what their concerns are, no matter how slight or trivial the concern is.

◇

◇

◇ **Tension on the neck or unconscious backscratching:** This behavior indicates serious doubt. When you notice this body language from a superior, for example, quickly pause and ask if something you have said in your presentation is out of order or amiss. They may help you get your facts straight.

All the above are signs that your client, employee, boss, or customer is about to object or reject what you are proposing or offering. To increase the chances of them listening to you until the end of your pitch or presentation, you should pause and address their concerns or give them the floor so they can also be part of the talk or share their concerns.

CHAPTER 13:
HOW TO WIN EVERY ARGUMENT

"That's the beauty of argument, if you argue correctly, you're never wrong." (Christopher Buckley, 1952, American writer)

BACK IN THE OLD DAYS, PHILOSOPHERS WOULD SKILLFULLY EMPLOY concise and pointed questions to exploit gaps in knowledge, enabling them to guide their disciples according to their reasoning. Engaging in persuasive arguments was considered a valuable skill and a true gift.

These days, we argue at work, with our spouses, friends, etc. We argue outside the courtroom, online, etc. Arguments are usually undesirable because people prefer to avoid losing or backing down. However, winning an argument can be a display of mental rigidity.

BUILDING THE FOUNDATION FOR WINNING

Individuals or speakers use arguments to persuade an individual or an audience about a topic. It involves appealing to reason with a touch of passion and emotion. An argument is better with a single individual because it helps tailor your points.

In establishing how to win an argument, I will explore the ancient trick employed by Aristotle. Aristotle used three modes of appeal: pathos, logos, and ethos. These three appeals to reason are a means to explore inner doubt in the opponent. It leverages a particular way of forming opinions.

Pathos has to do with the appeal to emotions. You aim to get your opponent to appeal to your point when arguing. A salesperson trying to convince a company to invest in a Fire extinguisher Ball could appeal to the emotion of the company's safety officer. Hence, he could say, "Investing in this Fire extinguisher Ball will improve your competency in the company."

Logos are an appeal to logic. Still, in the illustration above, he could recall facts that helped his cases. For instance, a Fire extinguisher Ball removes the extra expenses of servicing a fire extinguisher. The use of a Fire extinguisher Ball leads to saving money for the company. You must know who you are arguing with to use this approach. You need to see if they need facts or simple assurance. However, for Logos to yield, you need the points yourself.

Now here is where ethos comes in. Ethos, in this context, refers to the character and the arguer's credentials. Your point should possess enough legitimacy to persuade others to win an argument. In other words, you should establish yourself as an authority in the field. Let people see that you are knowledgeable.

HOW TO WIN AN ARGUMENT

Those mentioned above merely establish the foundation for the argument. Psychology has many branches which can help steer an argument in your favor — the human brain reasons well with logic, emotions, patterns, and numbers.

During the argument, emotion is a powerful weapon. Although exploiting emotions like panic and fear is purely diabolic or manipulative, feelings like vigilance are good. These emotions align with the human brain; if you can recognize them in your opponent, you already have the upper hand.

For instance, making eye contact during an argument might not help persuasion. However, this notion contradicts what many cultures have traditionally passed down about assertiveness – the belief that eye contact and a firm handshake help establish dominance. When trying to win an argument, however, you want cooperation and not dominance.

Eye contact is considered intimate and reserved for certain situations. Animals, for instance, will only make eye contact when they want to establish dominance. This behavior explains why dogs will make eye contact with each other before fighting.

You also cannot afford to show weakness. Your aim should be finding common ground with your opponent. Many studies have established that mirroring is a subtle way to build rapport. Hence you can mimic your opponent's body language and speech patterns—more of this in the next section.

Understanding and Mastering the Art of Arguments

In his book How to Win Friends and Influence People, Dale Carnegie advised that the best way to get the best out of an argument is to avoid it. He suggested strict avoidance of arguments as if they were the plague. However, viewing arguments as something to avoid strictly reflects a wrong understanding of their purpose, indicating an incorrect interpretation.

I only recommend the advice above if the argument also comes with a physical fight. Many people see arguments as a competition where one person stands with the trophy, and others get knocked out.

Having this mindset about arguments undermines reason. If you view an argument as a competition, then cheating will help you win. When adopting such an approach, interrupting people, persuading them with flawed arguments, and denigrating their views as ridiculous, stupid, or crazy are common tactics. You can even go as far as making a jest of their ignorance and their little knowledge. While this trick might help you win, it cannot help you understand their point.

There is, however, a better way to win an argument. Imagine you believe new moms should get up to six months of paid leave, and I do not. Seeing me as selfish and heartless due to our differing views on extended paid leave for new moms may make you consider me irresponsible.

We have failed to understand each other's views; hence, we don't respect each other. As a result, there is no ground for compromise or meeting points. However, suppose you support your assertion with the end: a six-month paid leave gives new moms enough time to bond with their little ones. I might counter you by saying employers will lose out if they pay for six months of work. This exchange of arguments and counterarguments allows us to understand our positions and acknowledge our shared values.

In reality, an argument doesn't go this smoothly. Failure to listen to our opponent or try to understand their reasoning deprives us of the opportunity of learning from them. A constructive and reasonable conversation where both parties express their opinion becomes hard when neither side gives any points to defend their position.

Failure to understand the point of an argument (to appreciate one another and find common ground) is why people tend to avoid it.

Furthermore, there is room for improvement in many arguments. People assume they give good reasons without really presenting anything. Hence, when people say things like, You're mistaken because you are ignorant. There is no basis for the conclusion reached.

No one benefits from jumping to such erroneous conclusions. Instead, the idea is to discuss and exchange ideas amicably. Analyze issues from premises to end. To do this successfully, you need the skill of proper and unbiased evaluation – how to differentiate a good argument from a bad one. Evaluation majorly involves sieving out wrong views and admitting reasonable statements. There is also a place for humility in an argument, as you must accept your weakness and acknowledge that the other party's reasons outshine yours. While you do not have to relinquish your conviction, your knowledge about the issue and your opponent would have increased.

Undoubtedly, the art of argumentation is a challenging task. The intricacy inherent in arguments is why the subsequent section will delve into the principles and guidelines of proficient argumentation. Your brilliant ideas are only valuable if you communicate them to the other party tactically and logically. Before I continue, I will discuss some dos and don'ts alongside clever tactics to twist any argument in your favor.

Dos:

◇ Stay Calm: No matter what, try and separate emotion from the argument. Don't lose your temper or get sentimental. If you do, you lose.

◇ Use Facts to Support Your Points: The salesman in the example above had facts. Hence, persuading the safety officer that the fire extinguisher balls were better than fire extinguishers was easy. Be sure to arm yourself with facts, statistics, etc. These make up the perfect arsenal that can help support your case.

◇ Ask Questions: Mastering asking a question in an argument can disorganize your opponent. They will scramble for answers, leaving them disoriented. Simple questions like where/what is your support for that claim? Employ the power of hypothetical questions as well. For instance, questions like: How will everyone be better off using this technique?

◇ Employ the Power of Logic: Employ the power of ideas following each other. Use this to build your case and see how it can undermine your opponent.

◇ Appeal to Higher Values: You can tap into the power of emotions by appealing to worthy causes or motives that are hard to disagree with.

◇ Listen Attentively: Many people are so fixated on what they want to say that they hardly listen to the opponent while arguing. When you look and listen carefully, you can observe the flaws and weaknesses in his stance. Besides, it could also be an avenue to hear something new and helpful.

◇ Study Your Opponent: Listen attentively and know their strengths, belief systems, values, and weaknesses. With this, you can appeal to their core values. You can also turn their arguments back to them, leveraging their faults.

◇ Be Ready to Concede a Good Point: Be sure to argue reasonably, not just for the sake of arguments. Admit and acknowledge all valid points that your opponent makes. To look reasonable and have the upper hand, outweigh it with another case. With this, you will appear reasonable.

On the other hand, we will also discuss some interesting things to watch out for and avoid while arguing.

Don't

◇ Get personal: Avoid attacking your opponent's lifestyle, integrity, honesty, etc. You are arguing on an issue, not their personality. Besides, avoid retaliating if the other party attacks you. It brings out your maturity and makes you reasonable.

◇ Get Distracted: It is easy to go off on a tangent while arguing. Your opponent might bring in extraneous ideas to counter your point. Make sure you are firm and you stay on course.

◇ Introduce Weak Points in Your Arguments: It is a good idea to focus on your strong points and leave out weak ones. Build on your strong points and make them very convincing so your opponent cannot refute them. More invalid arguments give your opponent a chance to weaken your entire case.

HOW TO WIN ARGUMENTS USING HUMAN PSYCHOLOGY

Arguments are frustrating as it comes with an overwhelming need to be heard and receive confirmation. Whatever the point of the argument, whether politics, religion, tribe, etc., no one likes the experience and sense of not gaining the upper hand.

Psychology has a way out for many people who can't find their way around winning an argument. These tricks will help you even if you are not good at debating. It will make people and your opponent see reason with your side.

1. Allow Your Opponent to Explain Their Thoughts First:

Be sure to ask open-ended questions encouraging them to explain their ideas and thought processes. Before you can have a successful argument, you must understand your opponent, their thinking patterns, and their beliefs about the whole discussion. Be sure not to interrupt them. Let them say everything they need to, as they will more likely pay attention to your rebuttals.

2. Mirror Their Body Language:

Remember, when mirroring, it is advisable to avoid being too obvious. Mirroring is a subtle way to gain your opponent's trust, which increases the chance of them paying attention to you. As subtly as you can, mimic their body language; cross your leg if they are crossing theirs too. However, be smart and not repeat every movement they make. The key is to appear as natural as possible otherwise, you will seem as if you are mocking them.

"Mirroring builds agreement; you can often head off potential trouble by establishing a strong basis of nonverbal agreement before the real negotiating begins," Nick Morgan.

3. Maintain Eye Contact When You Start a Conversation:

Be sure to maintain your gaze when your opponent starts talking. Psychology has established that this can weaken your opponent's persuasiveness. With this, you automatically have the upper hand when dishing out your points to counter theirs. Once they start talking again, be sure to make eye contact.

4. Repeat What You Think the Argument is About:

Always paraphrase what you believe their ideas and points are (as judged by what was said) before dishing out your counterpoints. With this, you build trust because it indicates that you have been following what they are saying, rather than waiting for them to finish talking, so you can get your points out. Making your argument persuasive becomes effortless if you want to gain your opponent's trust.

5. Acknowledge their Points:

To foster constructive dialogue, begin by acknowledging the valid points raised by your opponents and expressing agreement. By providing the rationale behind your agreement, you demonstrate respect and create an atmosphere conducive to considering differing perspectives when presenting your own arguments.

6. Know Your Facts:

Be sure you know what you are talking about even before speaking. Remember that the opposite party may ask you to expand or build on some points. You will just look like a fool if you can't explain yourself. Be sure you know your arguments like the back of your hand before presenting them. If you can't expand your points, there is a big chance of losing.

7. Keep Your Voice Down:

The last thing you want to do is raise your voice. Raising your voice will make the entire argument seem like a fight, preventing you from arguing reasonably.

With a calm, cool, and composed voice, your opponent will more easily trust you. Having a calm, cool, and composed voice has a high capacity to get people to consider your point.

8. Identify Common Ground:

Throughout arguing, it is essential to keep the atmosphere positive. Keep the dos and don'ts above in mind. Let your opponents know about the points that you agree with. Expressing points of agreement will likely make your opponent listen to ideas you disagree with and might encourage them to consider your perspective.

Getting into an argument can be intimidating, especially for people who don't like confrontation. However, subtle ways can improve your arguments and make your points persuasive. While you might not necessarily win an argument with these tricks, you will undoubtedly get people to listen and consider your point of view more.

With this, your confidence increases, and you can confront and persuade anyone.

CHAPTER 14:
BECOME A HUMAN LIE DETECTOR

"Every violation of truth is not only a sort of suicide in the liar but is a stab in the health of human society." (Ralph Waldo Emerson, 1803 – 1888, American Essayist)

IS SOMEONE LYING TO YOU? YOU DO NOT NEED TO TAKE a criminology class or be a high-class FBI profiler to be able to detect deception. However, detecting lying and deception is a skill many people are yet to learn.

At best, the chances of detecting a lie are 50/50, just like a coin toss. You could, however, develop yourself to put the odds of detecting deception in your favor. You could grow up and establish tips to identify lies with an accuracy of as much as 90%.

We will divide this part of the chapter into three sections:

Part 1: Have a model.

Part 2: Search for clues that vary from model behavior and show lying signals.

Part 3: Dig more profoundly for the truth if you feel you are being lied to.

PART 1: THE MODEL

The model is like the baseline or ideal behavior of the person in typical situations. In other words, the model's role in how they sound, talk, and react when they have no reason to lie is a crucial part of detecting deception.

In establishing the model process, ask questions about which the person would not want to lie. You could ask about their favorite meal or their favorite movie. During the process, pay attention to how they talk, their facial expressions, and their choice of words. Start with a physical model.

Part 1a: The Physical Model

Here, you will have to take note of all the physical characteristics shown during the conversation. You can approach it by breaking it down into various body segments. Be sure to take note of the following:

◇ The face
◇ The head
◇ The torso
◇ The arms and hands
◇ The legs and feet

Take note of the various body parts. During the conversation, what are they doing with their body parts? Are they continually touching their sleeve, their face, or rubbing their arm? Are they tapping their feet? What is the frequency? These are the models and characteristics you should watch out for. Hence, when the model part is over, you will look for deviations from these behaviors.

Now that you know their physical behavior when not stressed, let us get on to the next model.

Part 1b: The Audio Model

During the audio model, take note of their vocal pitch and how they sound during a normal conversation, a situation where they have no reason to lie. Be sure to take note of their tone, volume, speech patterns, word choices, word fillers, and gestures.

It doesn't stop at the physical and audio models; we must establish an emotional model. Developing an emotional model involves creating a framework for understanding how individuals' express anxiety, excitement, or nervousness about a specific issue. The weakness of "lie detectors" is their tendency to judge someone as lying, even when they are simply experiencing solid emotions or passionate about the subject of discussion.

Be sure not to pass on this step so you do not wrongly assume someone is lying when they are not.

Part 1c: Emotional Model

This part also involves asking questions. The difference, however, is that you will ask questions that will either get the person upset or excited. This approach will provide a physical and audio model of the person in an emotional state.

You could ask about politics, a day they will never forget, what caused their divorce or the loss of a kid, their favorite sports teams, or anything they are passionate about to get them excited. Ask them something that will likely upset them. The loss of a brother, sister, or a family member, their medical issue, etc., will make a good question (however, exercise caution).

With this, you get to observe and search for deviations in their behavior compared to the model you took of their "normal" behavior. For instance, when they talked about their favorite movie, their voice was filled with affection, more energy, and movement.

Also, it is likely when you asked about an issue that made them upset, they clenched their fist, might have stiffened up, or changed the pitch of their tone.

These are the baselines for the various conditions. The "ideal" model for them, whether they are excited or upset, is represented by this. Be sure to take note of variations and similarities in the baseline you took.

Model Complete

Model Complete marks the end of the model process. The idea is to make you understand the person under normal conditions when they have no reason to lie.

PART 2: LOOK FOR DIFFERENCES AND LYING CUES

In establishing if someone is lying, you should consider deviations from the abovementioned models.

If, while establishing the model, they gestured a lot, but their hands remained steady, it might indicate deception. It raises suspicion if they are clenching their fist, a behavior they didn't exhibit during the modeling stage. Consider it a red flag if their pitch suddenly becomes high, low, or hesitant.

These variations are clues you should watch out for. In addition to these variations, there are lying cues you should watch out for. These cues are huge red flags that reveal whether a person is lying.

◇ When the facial emotion contradicts the words said

◇ Nodding 'no' when saying 'yes' and vice versa

◇ Grooming and other self-soothing behaviors

◇ Touching any part of the face, like the nose or mouth

◇ Distancing or blocking behavior like touching the mouth or ears when speaking

◇ Long pauses and excessive use of filler words like hmm or ums when talking

◇ Excessive phrases like "to be honest with you..." or starting a statement with honestly...

◇ They appear to be thinking hard.

In the process of the conversation, you might have taken note of one or two red flags or clues. Take note of this.

Part 2b: Seek out Clusters.

A cluster is when you have three or more variations, red flags, or lying cues. As you converse, take note of the red flags and see if any of them fit as clusters.

Suppose you have a cluster for any response that indicates lying. Although, it might also be that the person is uncomfortable about a part of the conversation or hiding information. Whatever the case may be, you should examine this further.

PART 3: PRESS FURTHER

If during your discussion or, instead, investigation, you find clusters. You shouldn't just leave it. You should press further and dig more in-depth. However, what do you do exactly in this case?

You have got to decide what matters. Every day, we experience lies and deception in one form or the other from friends, co-workers, and family members. However, much of this doesn't matter. If it is not essential, you can choose to overlook it.

If it is important to you, and you need confirmation if they are lying, you should press further.

In pressing further, ask open-ended questions like "Could you please tell me more about…...?" or "When you said… what do you mean?"

With this, they get to talk more, allowing you to observe and establish your facts.

Finally, you can suddenly present them with a question and watch their reaction. If you come at them suddenly, you throw them off and destabilize them, so they have no choice but to reveal some truth.

This process will help to establish your lie-detection skills. Do not be disappointed if you don't find yourself being too skillful with this. A talent this worthwhile doesn't come on a silver platter. Researchers have extensively studied lying and deception, both prevalent human behaviors, over the years. While we understand that the above might take a while to master, some clear signs indicate that someone is lying.

Bear in mind that, at times, some people lie to protect other people's feelings. If a woman asks a man, for instance, "Am I fat?" And the man responded with a smile and said, "No, you are not." That could be a white lie meant to protect the other party. There are severe cases of lying (covering up a crime, for instance) in which the time to establish a baseline and model presented above might not present itself.

Over the years, researchers have strived to bring forth various ways of detecting lies. Although it is not very simple to tell if someone is lying, there are a few indicators.

FOOLPROOF SIGNS THAT EXPOSE A LIAR

As we discussed, relying on your instincts is fundamental when detecting deception. People often pay close attention to body language and various behavioral and physical cues to discern the truth from lies. Constant fidgeting, shifty eyes, and avoiding eye contact are typical signs that you are dealing with a liar.

Although body language cues could indicate someone is lying, research has shown that many of these behaviors don't involve lying. For instance, psychologist Howard Ehrlichman's study of eye movement revealed that eye movement does not necessarily mean someone is being deceptive. He suggested that shifting eyes could mean one is in deep thought or trying to tap into long-term memory.

Body language can be a terrific tool for detecting lies. However, it is essential to understand the signal you are going with.

What are the signals associated with lying?

1. They provide excessive detail:

A liar is never comfortable with silence, hence; they supply more unnecessary details than needed. You will get more information than you requested. Sometimes, just staying quiet might inconvenience the liar. Thus, they try to fill the silence with details to support the claim. Liars usually employ an excessive supply of unnecessary information to convince you and themselves to accept their deception. Additionally, liars often repeat a phrase multiple times to buy themselves more time to gather their thoughts.

2. They try desperately to be still:

While it might seem strange, being very still might indicate that a person is deceptive. The person's attempt to hide tension is the reason behind minimizing their body movements. Hence, you see the person pull their legs and arms towards the body, all because of pressure.

Think about it, in ordinary situations, people typically feel at ease and uninhibited, often displaying natural movements and freely expressing themselves. However, they might be rigid when trying to hide something fishy.

3. Their body language contradicts what they are saying:

Some people say they are fine, yet their body expressions and language say otherwise. At times, these people are even lying to themselves. In other words, their feelings don't match their words. Think of it as someone who frowns after saying, "I'm fine." – something is off. Also, pay attention to someone who shakes their head up and down while replying 'no.'

4. Changes in breathing:

Heavy breathing or a change in breathing pattern is a sign of nervousness. It could also be an indication that someone is hiding information. When people lie, it often triggers physiological changes such as an increased heart rate and altered blood flow, leading to heavier breathing as a reflexive response. Sometimes, someone lying might have trouble speaking due to the drying out of the mucous membrane in some parts of the mouth.

5. Change in patterns of eye movement:

People often say that the eyes are the window to the soul. While dealing with the notion that "the eyes are the window to the soul" in the context of lying, one must exercise caution. Using the eyes to detect lying is not about the direction of sight but a change in the direction. Therefore, when recalling information, certain individuals may look upward or downward while lying. Conversely, others may display different behaviors while being deceptive.

Be attentive to a change in eye movement. It is a strong indication of lying. However, know the person's model first (as explained in the previous section). The mentioned tactic is best suited for individuals you already know. A universal basis is that people who lie look at the door – because this is an unconscious escape route for them.

6. Making excessive pauses:

Making an unusual pause is a clear sign of lying. Individuals deliberately create a noticeable pause, allowing them to buy time for organizing their thoughts or constructing a compelling storyline. In trying to detect if someone is lying, be sure to take note of these pauses. They often hesitate and appear to be thinking hard to ensure that their stories have a flow and are believable.

7. They fidget:

Fidgeting, without a doubt, is a sign of negative energy. Experienced liars (except psychopaths) often fall victim to this as they are not sure you will buy their story. Hence, to let go of that nervous energy, they stroke their hair, play with their hands, tap their feet, and display other unusual signs. Shuffling the feet, for instance, is conventional negative energy associated with lying. The feet are unstable because the liar is uneasy, and the body is trying to escape!

8. Watch for Language Red Flags:

Watch out for distancing language, as liars might try to distance themselves from the lie. Watch for the use of pronouns as they speak. For instance, "I killed your chicken" could become "I killed the chicken." Liars often attempt to distance themselves from the subject of discussion, and using pronouns is a common way to achieve this.

9. Pay attention to the word "no.":

How does the person say the word no? Do they say no and look away? Do they say no and close their eyes briefly? Pause for a while and say no? Do they drag out the word and say nooooooo? Pay attention to all these clues.

10. Repeating the question:

While many would want to ensure they heard you right, a liar could be stalling for time. He might be trying to dig deeper and determine how much you know. Pay attention to these alongside other clues on the list.

Assembling all the Clues

For emphasis' sake, do not rush to conclusions. Be sure to know and understand what forms the usual and necessary behavior of this person in question. The signs of lying discussed above are meaningful when evaluated with the person's typical behavior.

If you are dealing with a victim of ADHD who fidgets easily, you can rule out some of these signs as lying indicators. Psychopaths also do not show most of these signs as they hardly feel remorse about lying.

Final Thoughts on How to Tell if Someone Is Lying

In conclusion, the reality is that there are no general and surefire signs that you can look at to confirm that someone is lying. All the indicators and pointers researchers have gathered over the years are just clues that can help reveal who is hiding something.

The next time you try to authenticate a person's information, don't focus on the signs of lying. Be sure to train yourself to pay attention to subtle behaviors that show deception. If possible, add pressure on the individual so that lying becomes mentally challenging. For instance, ask him to narrate the incident in reverse.

Lastly, as emphasized earlier, make sure to trust your instincts!

CONCLUSION

THERE IS A WEALTH OF INFORMATION ABOUT THE PEOPLE WE interact with daily that can tell us who they truly are and what they are currently thinking about as we interact with them. The challenge, however, is how to master the skills required to read this information.

Analyzing people may seem daunting, but even if you are not an undercover security agent, you can develop the skills required for reading people. Many people recoil when they hear the term "human psychology." It sounds too complicated a subject to be understood. But in this book, I have taken the time to present the skills to read basic human psychology in a straightforward way that anyone can understand. If you begin to apply what you have studied in this book, you will see how it is relatively easy to understand people and see them in a different light. It is like lifting a veil that has been covering your eyes for a long time.

I encourage you to drop all prejudices if you make any headway in accurately reading people. Equally, empathizing with others will significantly improve your chances of solidifying your business or personal relationship with them.

If you can practice these key lessons for a few weeks, you will notice a significant improvement in your career, business, and personal relationships. It is only possible to study how to analyze people by practicing it. That is why I encourage you to study this book more than once. Make it your companion until you have mastered your people-reading skills comfortably. The book may not have addressed your specific scenario, but you can apply the tips to any situation you find yourself in.

Finally, be discreet and "covert" about this whole reading people business. If you make it evident that you are trying to read people, you probably will not get any meaningful results. In other words, you must first master the body language of being secretive before you can effectively analyze people. After all, you cannot demonstrate what you do not have yourself.

Expect rapid positive changes in your career as you implement the ideas in this book.

REFERENCES

Dimitruis, J. &Mazzarella, M. Reading people: How to understand people and predict their behavior - anytime, anyplace. Retrieved February 8, 2019, from http://edition.cnn.com/books/beginnings/9807/reading.people.cnn/index.html

Bariso, J. An FBI agent shares 9 secrets to reading people. Retrieved February 9, 2019, from https://www.inc.com/justin-bariso/an-fbi-agents-9-ways-to-read-people.html

Cherry, K. Top 10 nonverbal communication tips. Retrieved February 9, 2019 from https://www.verywellmind.com/top-nonverbal-communication-tips-2795400

Lewis, J. Four types of business personalities. Retrieved February 9, 2019 from https://smallbusiness.chron.com/four-types-business-personalities-26162.html

Hubbard, R. Communicating with the four personality types. Retrieved February 9, 2019 from https://www.iidmglobal.com/expert_talk/expert-talk-categories/managing-people/staff_communication/id23383.html

Human metrics Inc. Determining other people's personality. Retrieved February 14, 2019 from http://www/humanmetrics.com/personality/ how-to-determine-other-peoples-type

Beckman Institute for Advanced Science and Technology. (2012). Science reveals the power of a handshake. Science Daily. Retrieved February 8, 2019 from www.sciencedaily.com/releases/ 2012/10/121019141300.htm

Clarke, G. The top 10 tips for the ultimate power handshake. Retrieved February 8, 2019 from https://www.europeanceo.com/business-and-management/top-10-tips-for-the-power-handshake/

Brooks, L. The Power of a Handshake. Retrieved February 8, 2019 from http://careerskillet.org/ the-power-of-a-handshake/

White, J. 6 Techniques for building rapport that will help you connect with anyone. Retrieved February 10, 2019 from https://www.learning-mind.com/ building-rapport-techniques/

Wood, C. 12 Body language signals only the best salespeople can read. Retrieved February 10, 2019 from https://www.nutshell.com/blog/ body-language-signals-sales/

Universal Class. Understanding body language in business. Retrieved February 14, 2019 fromhttps://www.universalclass.com/articles/business/understanding-body-language-in-business.htm

Goman, C. K. 10 Powerful body language tips. Retrieved February 14, 2019 fromhttps://www.amanet.org/training/articles/10-powerful-body-language-tips.aspx

Science of People. Office body language: 5 cues you must know. Retrieved February 14, 2019 from https://www.scienceofpeople.com/see-easily-can-master-office-body-language/

Farrington, J. How to deal effectively with objections. Retrieved February 9, 2019 from http://saleshq.monster.com/training/articles/230-how-to-deal-effectively-with-objections

Connick, W. How to handle objections in 6 easy steps. Retrieved February 9, 2019 from https://www.thebalancecareers.com/how-to-handle-objections-in-six-easy-steps-2917496/b

Kyle M. 3 scientific tips to detect lying. Retrieved February 10, 2019 from https://www.realmenrealstyle.com/lie-detection/

Kendra, C. How to recognize the signs that someone is

www.ingramcontent.com/pod-product-compliance
Lightning Source LLC
Chambersburg PA
CBHW031849200326
41597CB00012B/331